GAINING DAYLIGHT

Other Books in the Alaska Literary Series

The Cormorant Hunter's Wife, by Joan Kane (poetry)

The Rabbits Could Sing, by Amber Thomas (poetry)

The City Beneath the Snow, by Marjorie Kowalski Cole (short stories)

Gaining Daylight, by Sara Loewen (essays)

Upriver, by Carolyn Kremers (poetry)

Gaining Daylight

LIFE ON TWO ISLANDS

Sara Loewen

UNIVERSITY OF ALASKA PRESS FAIRBANKS

© 2013 University of Alaska Press
ALL RIGHTS RESERVED

ALASKA LITERARY SERIES
University of Alaska Press
P.O. Box 756240
Fairbanks, AK 99775-6240

Library of Congress Cataloging-in-Publication Data
Loewen, Sara.
Gaining daylight : life on two islands / Sara Loewen.
p. cm. — (Alaska literary series)
Includes bibliographical references and index.
ISBN 978-1-60223-198-6 (pbk. : alk. paper) — ISBN 978-1-60223-199-3 (electronic)
1. Loewen, Sara. 2. Alaska—Social life and customs. I. Title.
PS3612.O367G35 2013
814'.6—dc23
          2012033688

Cover design by Kristina Kachele Design, llc
Cover illustration: Akalura Window by Alf Pryor

This publication was printed on acid-free paper that meets the minimum
requirements for ANSI / NISO Z39.48–1992 (R2002) (Permanence of Paper
for Printed Library Materials).

 Printed in the United States on recycled paper

FOR MOM, DAD, AND PETER

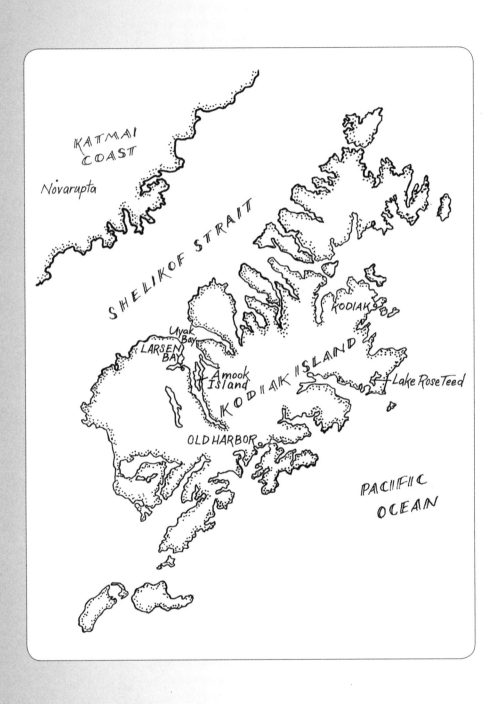

contents

preface

I would remain where I was and make the most of what I had.
—JOHN HAINES, *The Stars, the Snow, the Fire*

*To find a place that fits. Where past and present coincide. Where the
landscape feels like a version of the self. To walk out into such a place,
so at home in its vocabulary that you don't need words.*
—JUDITH KITCHEN, *Distance and Direction*

AS THE SUN RISES behind Amook Island, a heavy shadow of mountain slides
down the hillside into Uyak Bay. Light slips inside the cabin—old dog asleep
by the woodstove, sourdough starter on the counter, rain-soaked laundry
draped over every chair, Peter rushing for the teapot before its whistle wakes
the boys. We come here to commercial fish for salmon, spending the summer
on Amook, an island the size of Manhattan, population twelve.

My husband has spent thirty-four seasons at the fishsite. Fixing motors
and picking nets in rough seas is second nature to Peter, and I envy how
comfortable he is in this landscape. I arrived illiterate to winds and boats
and setnet fishing. Our young sons have crossed the bay hundreds of times.
Already, Liam and Luke are growing into the knowledge that gives Peter an

easy confidence in the skiff. I waver between feeling anchored here and feeling restless. "You lie as if you were in a cradle," wrote naval officer Pavel Golovin about traveling by kayak in Kodiak in 1861, "rocking from one side to the other...the waves wander through your hair, which is nothing, except that your eyes are full of salt water." Peace and discomfort in the same sentence.

When Golovin reported on the Russian American colony in Alaska, of which Kodiak was once the capital, he wrote in a letter home, "If it were not for the isolation from the rest of the world, and the severe climate, then it would be possible to live here. All the same, thank God I do not have to."

John E. Thwaites, delivering mail to Kodiak on the SS *Dora* in 1906, lamented in his journal, "Oh, for just one hour of warmth and quiet water!" A single hard winter on Kodiak in 1874 was enough to crush Icelander Jon Olafsson's plan to establish a colony here.

I was born and raised in remote Alaska, yet I am still adjusting to the isolation of a life surrounded by water, to days of slow rain that muffle sound and steal color. The Alutiiq word for sky is the same as the word for clouds. There are fishing seasons we've spent a year preparing for, and then the fish don't show up. We hope we can pay our mortgage and wonder what work might carry us through to the next good season. Kodiak is indifferent to prayers for fish or safe flights or for sunshine on a wedding day.

I sometimes wonder if people are born for certain landscapes, if we can't help being drawn to oceans or plains or mountains. I daydream of deserts and blue skies. Peter is at ease on the water. When we learned to scuba dive, he was relaxed and nimble underwater while I flailed and fought a pounding heart. Once, though, as I waited a few meters below the surface with a jumble of divers all clinging to the same anchor line, a sound I couldn't place made me glance up. A monsoon rained down above us, pounding the water with circles that struck and grew and began again. We were held in water under falling rain, untouched by the rain. In that moment, we witnessed the ordinary made new.

I picture Kodiak history like those growing circles of rain on the ocean—life stories overlapping, altering the adjacent circles, fading—especially as I walk on beaches still white with remnants of ash from Novarupta's 1912 eruption, or watch salmon returning to rivers in a cycle reaching back centuries. This archipelago holds the stories of thousands of years of Alutiiq culture, a century of Russian colonization, World War II bases and nets stretched between islands to snare Japanese submarines, the 1964 earthquake and tsunami that shook bears out of hibernation. Dozens of fisheries and canneries here have populated the town of Kodiak with families from Asia, Samoa, Mexico, and Central and South America. When Liam starts kindergarten in the fall, he'll be one of the few students in his class who speaks only English.

The ocean isolates Kodiak, but it has also carried visitors here for hundreds of years. When Natalia Shelikov traveled from Russia to Kodiak with her husband, Grigorii, to create a fur trading settlement in 1784, she brought along her two-year-old son and gave birth to a daughter on the trip. Newlyweds Victoria and Joshua Slocum spent time in Kodiak in 1871, well before he was famous for *Sailing Alone around the World*. Father Herman lived out his days on Spruce Island, becoming the first Russian Orthodox saint in North America. Even the Polish pirate Mauritius Augustus Count de Benyowsky claimed to have passed through Kodiak after escaping from Siberia on a stolen ship in 1771.

One of my favorite writers, E. B. White, ran into "thick weather" here in 1923 while aboard the steamship *Buford*. They were trying to deliver an Airedale terrier on one of Kodiak's zero visibility days. White wrote that a couple of ladies nervously asked whether "we shouldn't just drop anchor and wait for the weather to clear," noting, "This probably would have been one of the longest sea waits on record."

Throughout the 1700s, dispatches from Spain, Russia, France, and Britain passed through the archipelago—searching for the Northwest Passage, renaming landmarks, and claiming land for queens by burying coins and bottles with discovery dates and ship names. When Captain Cook sailed past Kodiak, poor weather frustrated his mapping efforts, and he mistook the island for mainland Alaska. "The difficulties came rather from frequent contrary, though strong, winds, and a combination of misty, drizzling and rainy weather that gave way to fog, fog that turned to rain and drizzle again," wrote biographer J. C. Beaglehole in *The Life of Captain James Cook*.

On that trip, Captain Clerke, commander of the HMS *Discovery*, called the Kodiak Archipelago, which stretches almost two hundred miles from the Barren Islands to the Semidi Islands and Chirikof, "a Labyrinth of rocks and

Isles." Amook is one of dozens of named islands in this group—Afognak, Sitkalidak, Raspberry, Tugidak, Shuyak, Uganik, Marmot, Spruce, Whale, Ban—and there are countless smaller islands dotting Kodiak's scribbled coastline.

I read recently that an archipelago can mean a group of islands, or the water around them, or a collection of corresponding things, like these stories about motherhood and marriage, writing, salmon fishing, and life on two islands.

GAINING DAYLIGHT

giant wings

IT WAS EARLY JUNE and Uyak Bay churned as fin whales and humpbacks feasted, heaving and gaping, and we watched openmouthed from shore. These whales eat thousands of pounds of krill and fish a day. When a pair of humpbacks breached over and over down the length of the bay, it drew me outside to where Peter was working with a couple of crewmen. We all yanked on our raingear and ran to the skiff, and then floated, motor off, farther from the humpbacks than the regulations require, as much out of fear as respect. Watching the whales breach side by side made the open boat feel like a leaf on the water.

I braced myself against the side of our aluminum skiff, the bulk of my rain-coat hiding six months of pregnancy. A surge of happiness surprised me. It was good to be on the water, to rush out into open space. Some days, overcast skies close over Amook Island like the lid of a box. I hadn't realized how lonesome the cabin had felt. I tried to think how many days it had been since I'd been off the beach. How many days since I'd felt happy.

A photograph of a breaching humpback isn't true. It is not loud like a bus plunging from a bridge. It's only the up, without the power of water to air, the startling grace, the enormity, the final slap. A photograph leaves out that deep secret beneath, water so dark and immense it can hide forty feet of whale, water that connects and carries these humpbacks from Kodiak Island in Alaska thousands of miles to the Hawaiian Islands or Mexico each year.

We spend winters in the town of Kodiak but leave every May for the salmon season, moving to our cabin in Uyak Bay on the west side of the island. At the fishsite we fall into a division of labor that feels both natural and restricting. When fishing is heavy, Peter is on the water more than he is on land, picking nets and delivering salmon. He is always moving, his attention pulled away from us and toward the bay. I take care of our sons, Luke and Liam, who are two and four and who love to be outside helping, which is why my garden vegetables grow in unruly rows and there is a permanent trail of dirt from one cabin door to the other.

When I stood facing Peter on our wedding day I said yes to this way of life without knowing the many things I was saying yes to. It's true of any marriage, that you can't know what you will gain or give up or the ways it will change you, but months on a remote island and the intensity of a fishing season can add to the magnitude of the choice. The fact that isolation can dredge up a loneliness you didn't know you were carrying around should be less surprising, yet it always feels wrong amid the beauty of an Alaska summer. It's the same as recognizing restlessness in the midst of a happy marriage or family life, or sadness you expected love to shield you from.

You'd think that living around whales every summer might eliminate the novelty or dampen the wonder. But their size alone is astounding. Inside fins almost two stories long are the same bones as a human arm and hand. I've read that humpbacks may carry a thousand pounds of barnacles; their hearts are as heavy as three people. Yet they are the lithest of whales, moving through the water as gracefully as "a swallow on the wing," in the words of nineteenth-century whaleman and naturalist Charles Melville Scammon.

Watching the humpbacks, I wanted to shed my sadness. I wanted to leap. The whales lifted and fell. They slapped their fins—the "giant wings" of their scientific name, *Megaptera novaeanglia*. Why the spyhop, the enormous back-stroke, the flinging rise to sky? It was comforting—the untidy questions left open, refusing answers.

Another June, a few years earlier, as I nursed my first baby at the cabin, I felt as content as I have ever felt at our fishsite, rocking Liam and watching the wind carry off the spouts of whales traveling out to Shelikof Strait. I can't help but attach tenderness to images of mother humpbacks lifting their newborns to the surface, though it might be anthropomorphism. A mother humpback usually won't let her calf travel more than a body length away. She'll some-times rest with the baby on her belly, or will rise up playfully with her calf on her back, letting it slide down her sides.

"The mother whale seemed solicitous only about her calf. She would fondle it with her huge snout, and push it along before her. She would get between it and the boats, to keep it out of harm's way," wrote Charles Nordhoff in *Whaling and Fishing* in 1856. "She would take it down with her, knowing that on the bottom was the safest place. But here the little one could not obey her. It was forced to come up to breathe at least once every two minutes, and by this means, even had we not been able to tell by the strain of our lines, we knew at all times where the old whale [was]."

I heard about a young humpback tangled in the seine of a local fishing boat last summer. The men on the boat said it cried like a wailing child as they worked frantically to cut away the net. Then its mother surfaced next to the calf, and immediately it calmed and was quiet. She stayed right there until her calf was freed.

When I cried over the news story of a starving baby humpback trying to nurse on the smooth underside of yachts in Sydney Harbor, I blamed the compulsive empathy motherhood seems to trigger. After all, it is not the same. The nipples of a nursing whale are more like a fire hose blasting gallons of pink milk into the calf's stomach, a hundred pounds a day of milk as thick as toothpaste.

So why do I think of them in the blackness under our skiff those nights we head home late, the baby under my jacket, me wondering if I was thrown into that cold water, if our skiff flipped, could I keep his head above the waves? Could I lift him into the air? I think of them those nights my babies root and nudge in the darkness and I meet them with an awkward turn, the ache of fullness.

Just after our second son, Luke, was born, I followed the humpbacks to Hawaii, inadvertently, when we traveled to Kauai for a friend's wedding. I was nervous about flying with a baby just a few weeks old. By the time our plane landed in Honolulu, my fingers had cracked from all the hand sanitizer.

"So what adventures do you have planned?" someone asked at the rehearsal dinner. Not zip lines, rafting, helicopter tours, or surfing lessons. It's an adventure getting two small children out the door and loaded into a car. These days are cluttered with an uneasy vigilance. Are they safe? Are they close?

In Hawaii, walking the beach around sunrise, enjoying the ease of slipping outside without a jacket or socks, I would search for spouts on the water, knowing somewhere offshore the humpbacks were giving birth and singing their lowing songs. Male humpbacks spend half the year singing. They sing alone and while escorting females with calves, and though every herd sings the same song, they make changes collectively as the season progresses. Jacques Cousteau described hearing humpbacks at night, their songs echoing off underwater canyons: "It seemed almost that one was in a cathedral, and that the faithful were alternating the verses of a psalm."

I would have liked to see our humpback whales again. But the boys were too little for catamarans and the baby too new to leave all day with a babysitter. They are still small enough that I can't imagine ever sending them off and letting them go. They fill my view. The only whales I saw in Hawaii were in a fountain at our Honolulu hotel—a sculpture of a mother humpback nosing her baby skyward.

When I next see humpback whales, they'll be in our cold waters. I'll follow two boys and two wagging brown tails down the beach. We are all visitors here, carrying within us our needs and songs, sharing the bay and these fleeting days of summer. Though the whales have been traveling since we finished the season, every year we watch them as if time hasn't passed, as if all is unchanged and stationary, the way you can't see your children growing while you are with them. From sea to sky, humpbacks breach again and again in Uyak Bay, and I watch, hoping to lift my own days to a place of contentment.

december

REMEMBER DECEMBER? RememberDecemberrememberdecember. My best friend was named for the month in which she was born. I loved the rhyme of her name and the way her hair, black as winter solstice, hung straight to the back of her knees. Braided, it swung out below her coat like a tail or thick rope, strong enough, I imagined, to hold an anchor. Sometimes I called her "Cem," which sounded intimate, the way using a family version of a name suggests closeness.

The village we lived in was a nickname place. The nicknames weren't just to distinguish boys from their fathers. Girls had them too. Lolly, Puddins, Sister, Choo-Choo, Dynx, Blondie, Fisherman. Nicknames set a child apart and also connected him or her to the place. In Old Harbor, grownups used the nicknames more than given names; the whole village did, so that those names sounded like belonging. I wanted a nickname. But they were for the children *of* Old Harbor and I was a teacher's kid, transplanted and temporary.

The nicknames were not the same as names that kids made up, say, for my older brother, whom they called "Mr. Rogers" to tease him for his whiteness. In Old Harbor, you might also be teased for dark features that looked too Native; it was mixed up that way. In 1784, this area on the southeast side of Kodiak housed the first permanent Russian fur trading settlement. Over the next century, the descendants of Russian men and Alutiiq women created a privileged Creole class within the Russian colony. Though that status diminished with the sale of Alaska in 1867, it may still have been preferable during American acculturation policies of the early 1900s. Later there were marriages between local girls and Scandinavian fishermen. Two hundred years of mixed heritage complicated the 1971 Alaska Native Claims Settlement Act for people on Kodiak when it came time to identify Alutiiq lineage to qualify for benefits. ANCSA helped revitalize Alutiiq culture through Native corporation funding for arts and language programs, but that shift wasn't visible in the 1980s when we lived in Old Harbor. December was Alutiiq, but it wasn't something I was aware of as a difference between us.

We agreed that everything should be the same between best friends, and so we dressed in matching colors and drew similar characters with the big eyes of *Garfield* comics and copied each other's handwriting until it was equally bubbly with circles above the i's. Same dolls, same favorite everything, same Halloween costumes, same dance moves choreographed to cassettes we played over and over, so that I still know all the lines from Madonna's first two albums and a surprising number of eighties hits for a girl raised without MTV—or television for that matter. From five to ten, those years of fierce imagination and play, I thought of December as my sister, even though I already had one. December is next to me in every birthday photo, every holiday recital. I was as sure of our sameness as I was that my baby dolls had feelings.

I willed my thin brown hair to grow, though it never reached much below my shoulders. When December got glasses, I was determined to get some too, so we would match in spite of my blue eyes. I prized having headgear because December had headgear. I actually chose to wear my headgear to school in third grade, until the recess when Alec Inga's hand tangled up with my face during a game of tag and tore out the whole apparatus. Old Harbor was a village without a doctor, much less a dentist or orthodontist. My dad—shop teacher and all-around handyman—found some pliers and pushed the metal brackets back onto my molars "for the time being."

Instead of nicknames, I settled for my parents' expressions like "skin and bones" or "slow as molasses." Praise or exasperation, it didn't really matter. I liked any label that seemed to distinguish me. Being the middle child and wanting attention made me do odd things, like pretending not to hear the beeps of a hearing test, or hooking my toes inside my snow boots so it took forever for my teachers to wrestle them off. I was proud of broken arms and the way I could fit a pinky between my crooked bite. The second time I broke my arm, we had to wait two days for the weather to lift before I could see a doctor for an X-ray and a cast. I relished those hours on the couch and the care with which Mom wrapped my arm in a splint made out of rolled magazines, and later, flying into town with Dad all to myself.

"Sara Peacock Cosmic Klutz," chanted Jack Christiansen when I came back with my arm in a sling. I didn't mind, it was sort of poetic, but I knew it wasn't a real nickname. Everyone called Jack "Yakoo."

Remember? How I never said no to you, December, even when you stepped in a puddle or dog poop and insisted that I step in it too because that's what best friends do. It might have surprised our teachers to know how you bossed me. You, who were so shy you wouldn't even speak in public. On school trips out of the village, I spoke for you in restaurants and stores.

"She needs to get over her shyness," teachers scolded. But I knew what you wanted by the way you moved your eyebrows. You were a whisper and I was your voice.

I have a memory without sound. The pastor stood in a chest freezer full of water; your parents must have hauled it into the middle of the kitchen the night before. I watched as if underwater, the whole baptism on mute. You stood facing me, with your bottom lip pushed out to the side, the way you always held it when you were mad or scared. I practiced that look a lot in the mirror. The pastor pushed you back and under the water and then jerked you upright. You came up streaming, wide-eyed and stiff as shale, your face and dripping dress the same shade of gray. Was it you or me who gasped?

On a Saturday morning—any Saturday, every Saturday—I waited in the doorway of December's house, frowning a little at my sneakers, which were hand-me-downs from my brother and too pointy in the toes to pass for girls' shoes. I crossed my arms, and then uncrossed them because it made my bony wrists poke out of the lavender sleeves of my coat.

"Can December play?" I leaned against the bags of dog food we often robbed for our "restaurant"—mixing cup after cup with water and feeding it to Puppers and Sukey until their stomachs bulged. December's mom nodded from the kitchen table, her hands busy with cigarette and coffee cup. I heard a story that once, late at night, she fell out of the skiff and her husband found her and fished her out by the orange glow of the cigarette still clenched between her teeth.

"Where you girls headed?" she asked.

"Playground," we said, but it didn't really matter. We might change our minds and ride over to one of the lots stacked with crab pots that we used as mazes and jungle gyms or wander to the beach to catch handfuls of jellyfish or climb the mountains behind school. It's hard for me to explain that freedom to people who didn't grow up there, even to my husband—how we weren't afraid of anything, how being so free made the whole outdoors ours. It's why I tell anyone who asks that it was the perfect place to be a kid. Maybe it's why I've never felt as sure of a place again. Old Harbor belonged to me, and then, in every place since, I've wondered, *Is this place home?* But it wasn't Old Harbor as much as childhood that made such ownership possible. And surely that feeling would have changed if we'd stayed. As a teenager I might have felt trapped or bored or uncomfortable in my white skin. And now, knowing how many schoolmates died early from accidents or alcohol, it's hard to reconcile such happiness with the luck of leaving in time. My best childhood stories start and end in Old Harbor. Sometimes we make a place, or a person, perfect by leaving.

To gain momentum on our bikes, we stood over the banana seats and pedaled straight-legged. We lived downtown, where the oldest houses were—rows of prefab housing hastily built after the 1964 tsunami destroyed all but two buildings in the village. When the houses were new, they looked so much the same that people occasionally wandered into the wrong one. Uptown was less than a mile away, yet we rarely rode our bikes all the way there, past the gravel runway and boat harbor, over the culvert where you could fish for silvers in the fall and ice skate in winter.

My eyes watered in the sharp breeze. The air tasted like woodstove smoke and smoked salmon. It made my stomach growl. I tried to spin gravel into the air but wasn't strong enough.

"If this bike was a BMX, I'd be a lot faster," I said, which reminded me again of finishing last in the Field Day bike race and how December didn't wait for me.

Last year I ran over a dog at the starting line of that race. The dog was exactly the size and shag of a janitor's mop. I'd always finished last in the Field Day bike race, but this time I positioned my bike near the front of the pack thinking that an early lead might make all the difference. Could there have been a gunshot to mark the start? Did that send him squealing into my path? Then I was falling—skinny limbs flailing, the sound of steel wool, the shame of this in front of a crowd. I clawed out from under my handlebars. The dog was fine; he'd already forgotten the mishap and was trotting away. I climbed back onto my bike and redirected my pity. It was hard to weep and pedal at the same time, but I managed a sad wobble down the race route.

I would have waited for December.

"You want to go tide pooling?" December asked.

"What?"

"CHICKENBUTT FRIEDINGREASE YOUWANTAPIECE?!?"

I hated it when she did that, but she thought it was hilarious. I would have been dead meat if I got caught saying something like that in front of my parents. December got away with more because she was practically an only child. Her brothers and sisters were older and lived other places. Later, it must have made the high school fights that much worse because her parents felt they were losing their baby.

Once, when we were fourth graders, we walked home together from a basketball game at the gym, a night so black the frost in the porch lights looked like spilled glitter. I breathed from the back of my mouth, trying to make my breath come out like cigarette smoke. A group of boys walked up—Travis and Jack and Emil and a couple more, about our age or a year or two older. Maybe they asked what we were doing and December said something like "none of your beeswax."

All of a sudden Emil lunged at December and lifted her into the air. He threw her down on her back and lay on top of her, pinning her as if they were two wrestlers while we all just stood there, stunned. She was crying and trying to push him off.

Emil stood up. Laughed through his crooked smile and walked away. The dark swallowed the boys. I tried brushing the frost off December's coat and pants. She started screaming every cuss word she knew.

"Sshhh, December, be quiet," I pleaded, more afraid of our parents' anger than of the act of a boy forcing a girl down against her will. "Your mom might hear you. Pleeeease." It was like everything that happened between them later started on that night, as if he claimed her on the ice.

I wasn't there for the years December and Emil were together. I moved to the town of Kodiak in fifth grade and by high school we'd stopped writing. I heard stories though, about the fights with her mom and dad because they didn't approve of Emil. Before that, her letters mentioned kids huffing gas on the beach, touching boys in the dark. I was years away from bras or boyfriends; maybe I felt that she left me behind. She may have felt the same way. We couldn't articulate the loss.

I didn't find December again until our thirties, via the Internet, that handy tool for confirming friendship long after it has ended. She's taking college classes. She has a little girl and is close to her parents. Though I've never met her daughter, it's her daughter's face—the youthful roundness and big smile—that is familiar. The years have sharpened December's features; she looks fierce even when she is happy. She is happy. I was so glad to learn that. I hadn't realized how my memories of Old Harbor held the absence of her.

When Emil died, violently, in the city of Anchorage last winter, it seemed like the ending that everyone expected. Hearing the news reminded me of another silent memory, although I know there was yelling and slamming doors. Emil was running down the elementary school hallway, away from the teachers and principal. I stepped out into the hall just as he reached the metal doors. He punched them open. Sunlight poured in and the light seemed to set his red hair on fire. I watched, six or seven years old, teacher's kid, knowing he was bad but quietly admiring. All the wildness that was not mine.

Each time December and I went to the beach, I would scan the ocean for signs of a tidal wave, just in case. My secret wish every time a tsunami warning sent the village up the hillside was for an actual flood, not just a few hours waiting out the warning before we all climbed back onto three-wheelers or walked home again. I didn't consider the loss of everything we owned. I just wanted to see the ocean floor bared, waves gulped back into Sitkalidak Strait by some invisible force, fish flopping, and mermaids clinging to rocks. I'd heard stories about the tsunami here, when villagers gathered on the hillside and watched a rush of water tow houses out to sea like boats, revealing the bottom of the channel as the water receded.

The last time December and I climbed that hillside we looked down at Old Harbor for a while and then kept climbing. Every peak revealed a new, higher mountain behind it. You couldn't see the continuing peaks from below, so these mountains surprised us. They beckoned. We hiked up and away from the village until the grass disappeared under snow. Our feet kept breaking through and we sank to our thighs. Then December spotted bear tracks, or maybe, she teased, they were the footprints of *Arula'aq*, the local Bigfoot. Some evenings, we kids dared one another to call the creature down by whistling to the darkening hillside. Now we scared each other into turning back, stumbling toward home through the brush and snow. When we confessed how far we'd wandered, we were both grounded. It was worth it. For the elation of discovering mountains, our believing that they went on without end, and that we could keep climbing one after another, together.

woman overboard

INTERNATIONAL CODE OF SIGNALS

From the Oxford Companion to Ships and the Sea

A signal lamp, also called an Aldis lamp, produces a pulse of light for ships to communicate using Morse code in times of radio silence. The idea of flashing dots and dashes from a lantern was first put into practice by Captain Philip Colomb in 1867.

• •

I AM ALTERING MY COURSE TO PORT

For half the year we give up fresh produce, telephones, cars, dryer, and dishwasher. We pack up the boys and the dogs and buy a season's worth of groceries. To get supplies to the fishsite, we fill and label boxes and totes and deliver them to a boat in Kodiak, which carries them around the island to the village of Larsen Bay. We pick them up at the cannery, haul them down the dock, skiff them across Uyak Bay, and then heft them one by one up a slick jumble of beach rock, over the rise of beach grass and driftwood, and then up the steep hillside. We unpack and settle in for the salmon season.

·· _ ·

I AM DISABLED—COMMUNICATE WITH ME

I can see Peter pulling up to the net as he calls on a handheld VHF. He can't hear my replies. I walk outside and wave a second time from our cabin deck and leave the door open when I go back inside. A few minutes later I hear him shouting my name.

I remember this overzealous policeman dad who, picking up his son from the school where I taught, would lecture the kids on the playground about screaming. "Shouting should be reserved for obtaining help during a dangerous situation," he scolded. "It shouldn't be part of recess play."

"Good luck with that one, buddy," I thought.

But maybe he was right. Every time Peter hollers my name from the beach or his boat, my heart stops and I run for the door. Is he being mauled by a bear, has his skiff flipped, did he lose a crewman to the waves, did he accidentally cut off a finger, did he lose his lucky hat? No. Today is the first day of salmon season and he's so excited he's shouting from the skiff. His voice rides up on the wind. "Sara!" He points and yells, "Reds in the net!"

_ ··

KEEP CLEAR OF ME—I AM MANEUVERING WITH DIFFICULTY

No need for signals. My husband knows this look. This is the look after a night like this: Climb into bed at midnight, already looking forward to coffee in the morning. It's June, which means the sunlight is still bouncing off the ceiling in spite of double curtains over the windows. We all sleep in the loft of our cabin so we don't bother with sleep training out here. I'm pretty sure the "cry it out" technique requires doors and separate bedrooms. Also, a crying baby, which, to be honest, I couldn't bear even if we had doors that closed. Which means it is all my fault when the baby wakes up hungry at 2:00 a.m. and happily nurses his way through to morning. At 4:00 a.m. I hear Liam crying, "Mama, I want to snuggle. Maaamaaaa." Peter doesn't wake; he sleeps heavy as a sea lion during the fishing season. Liam climbs into our bed. "I need a pillow!" I give him mine and sink back into a half sleep.

— • — —

I AM DRAGGING MY ANCHOR

The writer Ron Carlson tells his students, "When you sit down to write, whatever you do, don't get up for a cup of coffee." But I'm pretty sure he isn't up all night with a baby who is not a self-soother. I don't think Ron's daily planner reads: change diapers, pajamas to clothes, cook pancakes, read stories, nurse baby, make pizza dough with toddler, sweep up flour, wipe egg off cupboards, fix snack, paint, clean up paint, feed baby, play with blocks, build pirate ship, fix lunch, hang laundry out to dry, water garden, puppet show, hide and seek, make tree fort, change diapers, read more stories, naptime! Race to the computer. I *need* this cup of coffee in a way Ron Carlson could never understand.

• • • •

I HAVE A PILOT ON BOARD

I watch Peter steer us home in the skiff. His ears are peeling. His red beard and cheeks are flecked with jellyfish parts and silver scales under a sun-bleached ball cap stiff from days of saltwater and slime. He smells like salmon blood and sweat. His hands have swollen too big for his wedding band; his palms are Portobello mushroom thick. He is so at home in this place it's as if he leapt out of the bay and landed in this skiff. I am full of love, so much love it could sink me.

— •

NO (NEGATIVE)

On our wedding day, I wasn't thinking about the fishsite as we said our vows. I wasn't thinking of work I once considered old-fashioned—hanging laundry on the line, baking bread, hauling firewood, waiting for the hum of Peter's skiff to put dinner on the table. I was thinking of old boyfriends and how I could only have sex with one man for the rest of my life. But thanks to salmon season that rarely happens anyway.

— — ·

I REQUIRE A PILOT

The thing about marrying a fisherman who "comes home at night" is that night might start at 1:00 a.m. Mornings start at 5:00. There is no such thing as a weekend. The drawback to marrying a capable, cheerful person is how much you miss them when they're not around.

— — · —

MY VESSEL IS HEALTHY AND I REQUEST FREE PRATIQUE

the first red salmon on the grill
the smell of beach fires and cottonwood and tomatoes in the greenhouse
whales out the window
orange poppies
rhubarb pie
such luck, to live on this island

— —

MY VESSEL IS STOPPED AND MAKING NO WAY THROUGH THE WATER

Peter stands up midway through lunch, scanning the water with binoculars.

"They're out there. They're not showing, but they're out there." He swigs his coffee as he paces the living room.

Friends often ask how he does it. How he can stand the fatigue and monotony of all the long days of pulling on wet raingear and stinking boots, hauling nets against the waves or wind.

He says, "If you had a tree that grew money in your backyard, wouldn't you want to keep on picking it? Wouldn't you go out there until you'd gotten every last dollar? I think of it like that." Out here he is the provider, the captain, the muscle. And he gets all the glory.

My aunt and uncle visited a few weeks after Liam was born. I cooked and washed dishes with the baby in a front pack. When they boarded the float-plane to leave a week later, my aunt said, "You married a good man, Sara." I agree. He's good-natured even when he's tired. He's smart and handy. When he does something for the first time, from building a house to wiring a cabin for solar panels, he reads and teaches himself how to do it. But sometimes, watching him leave from the shadow of the cabin, I think of the upcoming hours of mothering and cleaning and cooking and baking. I am not going anywhere. I feel a little jealous.

_ • • •

I AM CARRYING DANGEROUS GOODS

Liam just realized as he peed off the back porch that he needed to go number two. He ran for the bathroom. I think we've reached a turning point. A week ago he would have done both number one and number two on the porch and I would have praised him and cleaned it up, convinced it was preferable to cleaning poop from his big-boy underpants.

From the back porch, I spot some other number two, courtesy of the dog, near my garden bed and try to chopstick it up with two sticks and fling it into the alders. It catches on a branch under the bird feeder. I didn't think that was possible with dog turds, but Schooner eats a lot of grass out here. Poop is something I didn't plan to spend so much of my thirties talking about or praising or examining or cleaning up.

"Did you go poop?"

"Yep. I did."

"What are you eating?"

"Dog food. Dog food is my favorite."

• • _

YOU ARE RUNNING INTO DANGER

"Liam, give that toy back to your little brother. He's just a baby. He can't help drooling on things. Liam, give that back now. I'm going to count to three. You have to trade him with another toy. There you go. Wait. He can't have marbles. That's better. Hugs are nice. Gentle.... That's enough. Off. Get off your brother."

• _ • •

YOU SHOULD STOP YOUR VESSEL INSTANTLY

"I SAID, GET OFF YOUR BROTHER."

— — —

MAN OVERBOARD

Out we go. We are abandoning cabin, heading for the beach. We are going to build a castle. We settle into the peaceful rhythm of collecting. Luke stuffs chubby handfuls of sand into his mouth. Liam finds white rocks, purple mussel shells, beach glass, driftwood. He fills the moat with water. I admire what we have made.

— • • —

STOP CARRYING OUT YOUR INTENTIONS AND WATCH FOR MY SIGNALS

As I climb into bed, Peter wakes up, sleepily horny, and reaches for me with hands like sharkskin that catch on my pajamas. He'll be snoring again within twenty-six seconds. "I love you. Goodnight." Nothing sounds better than sleep.

Sleep.

— • — •

YES (AFFIRMATIVE)

to know a place

TO BUILD OUR CABIN on Amook Island, we dug through five feet of midden. When shovel met rock, we buried the pilings—leftover tops of Douglas fir logs from cannery docks in Larsen Bay—and framed our cabin over heaps of refuse. Sometimes I dig my fingers into layers of sharp, flat shale and pull clamshells from between rock and bones. Inside the smooth white bowls are ash, berry seeds, the green powder of crushed sea urchins, and fragments of lavender mussels. We built on a picturesque dump.

This morning I climbed down from the loft and looked out at gray sky and water; the cabin still in the mountain shadow that sunrise washes toward the shore. By midsummer, this hillside is a dense green too thick to hike, except for a crater of exposed rock from an old landslide that carried tub-sized boulders a thousand feet to the beach. A caramel movement caught my eye. A bear sat on the ridge. Both of us taking in the view.

Who else has shared this view? Watched the sun set in June as if it was following a game trail along the mountains across the bay? A disappointed gold
miner who left dishes and a rusted bed frame that we hauled from the creek.
Alutiiq families who gathered the shells and bones that sift and settle under
my garden beds and raspberry patch.

Uyak is surrounded by five thousand years' worth of Alutiiq settlements—
a reminder that we live by our bellies. People stayed here for the food that
washed in with tides and seasons, for the traffic of otters, seals, sea lions,
whales, and fish. To the west, millions of salmon once returned to the Karluk
River. Halibut and cod wander beneath sockeye and humpies skipping into
the air and up the bay. Daily, the sea steps back with a waiter's flourish. Butter
clams, octopus, littleneck clams, cockles, mussels, limpets, whelks, urchins,
chitons. A salad of seaweed is strewn along the beach—brown, popweed, bull
kelp, and ribbon. There's an old saying on Kodiak: *When the tide is out, the
table is set.*

We are here from spring to fall, during the richest harvest time. Yesterday I heard hammering from the front porch and found Peter trying a new
technique for cleaning sea cucumbers. He stretched the animal between two
nails and cut out the five long muscle bundles. Pencil thin and toffee colored,
they stretch like foot-long rubber bands. We catch sea cucumbers when they
tangle with kelp in the lead lines of our salmon nets. In the skiff, they heave
out their guts so that predators will eat the feathery insides and leave the sea
cucumber to grow new entrails. These animals were traditionally harvested
during minus tides by hand or with spears tied to long poles. Pete cooks the
strips in olive oil. The meat tastes brackish and sweet. I think of the care and
labor to produce these small crisp bites, and it seems that food, as much as
landscape, connects us to the people who first chose this place.

When Liam was a year old and just beginning to walk, I marveled at the way
he mimicked me on the beach. As I loaded wood or seaweed into the wheelbarrow, he found his own small sticks and kelp to add. Now he wants to "cut"
fish the way he has seen us filleting. His response to most sea creatures is "I
eat that." Picturing children who must have helped gather the mollusks and
berries and eggs in these midden piles, I feel closer to the oldest kind of learning and teaching: every task a preparation. The toys found in archaeological

digs around Kodiak are miniature versions of stone knives and women's tools, or spears and tiny boats with paddles.

On stormy mornings I turn the VHS to channel six and listen for impending weather. Out here the sky and ocean are one great body, each full of the other. We don't mind a southwest breaking on our beach because it seems to bring the salmon in. Wind from the northeast might bring rain. In Larsen Bay the northeast that arrives with a falling tide creates a swell, and old-timers there call it *qalli'iq*, the noisy woman's wind. Alutiiq families often had sitting areas on their sod roofs for weather forecasters who advised hunters in the morning on which way to paddle in order to return with the wind at their backs.

Wishing to know a place, we note weather patterns and the change of seasons. We memorize the names of birds and trees and teach them to our children. In May, the cottonwoods on Amook Island unfurl to the song of thrushes and chickadees. We build and garden. All summer I pull nettles and put roots down into the ground, transplanting mint or burying perennials that the foxes mark in the night. In the fall I blanket it all with seaweed and wrap the lilac tree against the deer as if finding it alive after a winter will make this place more my own.

A yellow leaf on the beach catches my son's eye. "Mama, what's that?" he asks.

"It's a leaf," I say.

"No," he says and shakes his head. He doesn't recognize it. Leaves are green.

Fall should bring the relief of a busy season ending. We'll have time together as a family again, once the nets are mended and cleaned, the buoys pulled, the totes and gear stacked, the motors winterized, the skiffs stored, the cabins boarded. When I read about the seasonal moves of Alaska Natives, it sounds natural and sensible. Yet we come here in the spring and leave in the fall, and every year the transition feels just as abrupt and difficult. I never feel at ease closing up and leaving either home for half a year.

Now fall has arrived and I'm still waiting on carrots, parsnips, and peas. I can't welcome the darker blues of September storms, the stronger winds, or the wet peppery smell of weary plants. I ignore the fading pink sheet of fireweed on the hillside. Before we leave, we dig up our potatoes. We package salmon and halibut for the freezer, shoot and butcher deer for a winter's worth of venison. The teapot is always whistling now. I bake with winter flavors like cinnamon and cloves, and with sticks and sticks of butter. The cabin smells like the walls are built of gingerbread.

What scents drifted through the skylight of a sod house? Smoke from seal or whale oil burning in stone lamps. The smell of food roasted on a hearth or cooked in clay pots, steam rising with the addition of each hot stone. To get through the winter, Alutiiq families dried their summer catches of halibut and cod. They smoked salmon. They filled seal stomachs with oil and berries and stored fish eggs in bark boxes and plants and roots in grass baskets.

"They treat their visitors, upon first entering their dwellings, with a cup of cold clean water," wrote Martin Sauer on a 1788 Russian expedition to Kodiak. "When they have rested a while from the fatigue of rowing or walking, they put before them whale's flesh, the meat of sea lion, fish, berries mixed with oil, and boiled sarana, also mixed with fish oil, and it is expected that the guest eat all that is set before him. In the meantime their bath is heated, and the guest is conducted into it, where he receives a bowl of the melted fat of seals or bears, to drink."

I imagine a woman—hundreds of years ago—leaving the dark warmth of sleeping bodies, stooping through the low entrance to rise into this cold fall wind. She would have looked out over the protected beach to where the bay spills toward the white ridge of mainland Alaska. From here she could see the kayaks approach. She'd recognize those of her family members. The tattoo on her forearm—drawn with seagull bone and charcoal—matched her husband's boat. She would have helped to sew the covers, stretched the skins over the wooden kayak frame slicked with seaweed.

I appreciate our vantage point. From the cabin I can see boats approaching with time enough to start a pot of coffee for company or to pull on boots and meet visitors at the running line. Yet this site was not first chosen with hospitality in mind. The hill provides a defensible lookout, a quality the Alutiiq people valued as much as living near salmon runs and fresh water. Warfare was common between neighboring tribes and settlements. They fought for trade goods and slaves, or for revenge. They fought against the first Russian fur traders who arrived in the late 1700s but lost to cannons and muskets and then to epidemics of smallpox, measles, and influenza. Half of Kodiak's population died between 1784 and 1814, writes Craig Mishler in *Black Ducks and Salmon Bellies.*

Across the mountains from the head of Uyak Bay is Three Saints Bay, where, in 1784, Grigorii Shelikov crushed Alutiiq resistance at a site called Refuge Rock. The Russians killed hundreds of men, women, and children who had gathered on a small islet. Then Shelikov took hundreds more captive, the start of a system of forced labor under the Russian-American Company that lasted almost a century. The Russians called the islet Razbitoi Kekur—*kekur*, from the word for "offshore rock," and the verb *razbivat*, "to break or defeat." The Alutiiq people called the islet *A'wauq*—to become numb.

Our days here are set to the sound of gulls protesting hungry jaegers and eagles and to the steady violence of wind and waves wearing away at the edges of the island. When Peter recently towed the carcass of a large sleeper shark off the beach, it seemed somehow wasteful. But foxes had been feasting on the carcass, and we thought that bears would come next. He tied a line to its tail and pulled it toward the middle of the bay, then around the corner of Amook Island. In the morning it had washed up a meter from where we'd first found it.

Alutiiq whalers relied on such currents to deliver whales to the beach. Whaling shamans mixed poison for their spear tips from monkshood root and fat rendered from human corpses. Once speared, the whale usually died within a few days. When a dead whale washed onto shore, it was claimed according to the whaler's markings on the spear tips. That was a rich man, who could provide and share so much valuable oil and meat. I've read descriptions of objects—amber and abalone, multiple kayaks, fur parkas, sea lion skins, stone lamps, and baskets and bentwood boxes full of food—that demonstrated wealth for Alutiiq families on Kodiak before the arrival of Europeans.

Last night I filled the old drum stove with wood and cardboard and lit the *banya*—a blending of Russian saunas with Alutiiq bathhouses: side huts carpeted in fresh grass where bathers poured water over heated rocks. A friend was visiting, and we washed the kids in the dark, hot room. Steam hissed off the cedar benches and the round beach stones piled around the wood stove. Clean and content, we stepped out onto the banya porch into the cool autumn air. We are rich in driftwood. Rich in fish. Rich in wind and blue tides.

capacious

THE CABIN AT OUR FISHSITE has a high ceiling and might feel spacious if we could flit like birds through the air above our heads. On stormy days the antonyms apply: *cramped, tiny, squeezed*. Like finding the time to write. Or sharing a bed with a Labrador, six-feet-something of husband, and a two-year-old who prefers to sleep diagonally. Most nights I hold myself in place with one hip anchored to the wooden bed frame.

Summer in Uyak Bay is cold wind and waves. The silver glint of salmon sloshing in totes of ice. I crave a desert summer. The bright heat, hard rain, lightning fading to a muted evening. But because a northern June offers generous light in place of warmth—when it isn't soaked up by fog and storms—I still think of summer as the most capacious season.

I find myself subscribing to impractical magazines, hoping to share in that *other* summer unfolding far away from our cabin. But sometimes the stone fruit recipes and photos of garden parties start me lusting after sweet juicy peaches enticing birds in orchards and plums and nectarines and cherries rolling fat and tender out of grocery bins. All my favorite fruits ripening to perfect luscious mouthfuls, and I am missing it.

I settle for poems soft between my teeth. Lee Young-Li's

...succulent

peaches we devour, dusty skin and all,

comes the familiar dust of summer, dust we eat.

O, to take what we love inside,

to carry within us an orchard, ...

This year I planted a small cherry tree hardy enough for our constant winds, for the fruit and for the rosy June blooms.

◎◎

Capacious ends with a wet mouthful of sounds. Ends with *sh* and *s* like the feel of a skirt swishing against bare legs. A feminine word to rhyme with flirtatious, curvaceous. Not a wanton word. The word wants to be good.

Capable of containing a large quantity, spacious and roomy: *she rummaged in her capacious handbag.* A little like pregnancy then—for the baby in the womb—not the mother.

Motherhood, pregnancy—nouns not big enough to hold both the gift and the burden. I aim for synonyms. Abundant gratitude. Comfortable in this way of life. Generous with affection. Can I make a place of calm in this world? Be that place?

I aspire to the idea of a capacious life, but I feel foolish trying to grow spiritually, to make my thoughts more expansive after reading some meditation book or an *Oprah* article. I struggle just to use the word in a conversation.

"If we had a nanny I think I could be more capacious," I say to my husband.

"What?"

"I think I could be more capacious."

"What's capacious?"

"You don't know? Darn. I was trying to see if I used it right."

A full life. *Able to contain a great deal; affording much space.* As in *a colonial fire-place capacious enough to roast an ox.* But of course, in saying that I hope to live fully, I mean that I am hoping for a life full of good.

"It just means that I'm going to lead an interesting life," I once told my older brother when he noticed the excessive lines on my palms. My handprints are like cracked mud, a fractured windshield.

"Well, you'd better get started then," he replied.

Lately, my son Liam has been begging for one bedtime story over and over. One based on a true story that I only planned to tell once. What's that old joke? Where does the lion sleep? Anywhere he wants to. And on our island, where do red foxes poop? On any claimed space, on every path and flowerbed and berry patch. This is the story my two-year-old adores. The time the foxes pooped on the ___ (insert any item here). When he asks for the story again and again, I scold myself for encouraging potty humor. Until I hear him laugh. The last of the baby is there in that sweet and flawless sound. I would say anything, tell any story for that sound. I would do anything to make room for laughter in his life as he takes in the good and the terrible of a world big enough to hold all of it.

This fishing season and my second pregnancy will both end by October. I have to stop now to catch my breath when I carry Liam up the hill from the beach. When I heave myself into our skiff and we lift and fall over the swells, I wonder if the baby notices the water's motion or if it's all the same to him. Waves inside and outside. I've become a vessel. A sea beside the ocean.

unsinkable

I GREW UP AROUND BOATS, but it was my older brother, Reuben, who learned how to drive a skiff and repair an outboard motor. On family fishing trips when we were kids, my sister, MaryBeth, and I were content to trail ribbons tied to CareBears or My Little Ponies in the wake. I rode in the bow with canine enthusiasm, gulping in wind that tangled my hair into knots that could not be combed out. It was exhilarating just to be going, to be moving over the waves. This was one reason I asked for a skiff of my own after my first season at the fishsite. I wanted the feeling of going. And there is another reason. Although I'm not yet confident on the water, I want our children to grow up riding in Mom's boat too.

This summer—my third season in Uyak—I got my first skiff, a seventeen-foot 1960s Boston Whaler with a two-stroke sixty-horsepower Yamaha. Before her retirement ten years ago, she was one of the main fishing skiffs at our setnet site, hauling hundreds of thousands of salmon. This was the first skiff Peter worked from as a full crewman when he was thirteen. He remembers salmon floating around his boots when they picked the nets in rough seas. The sides are low, and when waves broke over the bow they sometimes washed fish out of the transom. Now we fish from large aluminum skiffs that can hold more and are better suited to our rocky beaches. When Peter hauled the old Whaler out of the beach grass, she needed a few repairs. The crewman who did much of the fiberglass work used to make surfboards in California; he treated the Whaler as if she were a longboard instead of a fifty-year-old boat. She's watertight and solid, but she could use a paint job. The skiff is aqua with yellow fiberglass patches on her hull that make me think of roller skating knees.

I was nervous when I first took the skiff to Larsen Bay. "You're sure it won't sink?" I asked Peter.

"You could chainsaw this in half with a person sitting in both ends, and they would both keep floating," he said. "This skiff could fill with water and it would still float." I wish I didn't know that his information came from old Boston Whaler commercials—*Boston Whaler, The Unsinkable Legend!*—but I figured this trip had to be smoother than my past attempts in other boats. The first time I was alone in one of our aluminum skiffs was during a gale. We were driving two skiffs side by side, but Peter anticipated and adjusted for the waves while I clung to the steering wheel and managed to plow into each one. It was like aiming for potholes. Water knocked my hood back and streamed under my raingear and into my boots. I'd been scared when we started out, but pretty soon that changed to fury—at each dousing of icy water, at the fear knotting my stomach, at the storm, at Peter, at this place where even going home at night was hard.

That same summer, on a clear afternoon, I'd made my first solo crossing of Uyak Bay. I hadn't been off of Amook for days and was motivated by the thought of visiting with my mother-in-law, Jan, to talk about books over a cup of coffee, to talk about anything, really, with another person. I pushed a camouflaged duck-hunting raft off the beach and jumped in. Earlier in the week, my father-in-law had assured me of its seaworthiness and then shared a story about towing it behind the skiff one October and looking up to see the raft soaring like a kite behind the boat.

I had one passenger—Schooner, our chocolate Lab, riding in the bow. To steer with the tiller handle required perching on a tubular side a few feet from the ocean. That was fine in calm water, but by the middle of the bay, the waves grew too big to see over. Suddenly the little raft felt more like an inflatable wading pool. I was afraid it would flip. I couldn't predict the next roll of ocean. The swells were disorienting. My in-laws were surprised to see the raft across the water. They would spot it, and then it would disappear a while before bobbing back into view. Schooner paced with his tail between his legs. I'd gone too far to turn back. "No way out but through," I recited, in between praying and hollering at the dog to sit down.

Sometimes during a particularly rough skiff ride, I try to imagine how it would feel in a kayak, and I think of Hieromonk Gideon's account as he inspected Kodiak for the Russian Orthodox Church in 1804. "My heart was filled with sorrow: after calm weather and fog, a strong, most cruel wind arose accompanied by adverse current. The paddlers tired, the weather grew worse. The swells constantly rolled over us," Gideon wrote. "From great exertion, blood spurted from the noses of the paddlers. We expected imminent destruction. God be praised, we reached a deserted shore—but just barely."

When I head to the village of Larsen Bay in the Whaler, I drive slowly until the butterflies sink. I pass the channel markers and hear my brother's voice from a sailing trip in college, "Red, right, returning." I pass the Russian Orthodox Church and Frenchie's Point, where crows are rising off the bluff like bits of ash from a campfire. Driving the skiff is like coasting a bicycle down a long hill or kicking toward blue sky on a swing set. It gives me back the feeling of freedom I've missed.

Outside the cabin windows, my skiff nods from the mooring line as the changing season shows in stronger wind and waves. Soon we'll put the skiffs away for winter. With her engine fogged and flushed, the Whaler will sit dry in the warehouse until spring. Next summer I'll take my son beachcombing or berry picking in this skiff. On the way to his grandparents' cabin, we'll look for otters and seals at the haul-out rock. I'll take my dad and mom fishing when they fly out to Uyak for a visit.

There is a fist pointing forward on the bow that a crewman painted in the eighties. It points in various directions depending on the wind. This way to Katmai. This way to the head of Uyak Bay, with its Kodiak bears, dark as molasses. This way to Cape Town, Sydney, San Francisco, Shanghai. I would never venture as far as Shelikof Strait, but I like thinking about the ocean we share, traveling on an element that moves with the sky and moon and the earth below it. No lanes, just always changing open space.

After the salmon season ends, we like to stay a month or so out at the site. There is still work to do, but a kind of quiet settles around the bay. The radio goes silent after the fishing boats and setnet families have stored their gear and left for winter homes. In the fall the light is soft and everything else is crisp— the breeze and night skies and the sharp smell of herbs when I empty pots into the garden. We remark on the changes in wildlife that seem to signal the impending winter—the halibut aren't in the same spots, the bears are coming around more often. We spend a day watching humpback whales breach just a few hundred yards from the cabin while a pod of orcas circle the bay. When Peter points out the arrival of ducks migrating overhead, Liam responds by pointing and mimicking his favorite bird this summer, "Chickadee!"

The Pekars were our last visitors this year. They brought their new baby, Henry, a cooler full of fresh fruit and vegetables, bottles of wine. We're lucky our family and friends don't mind the work of getting to Amook Island—the hour flight to Kodiak, another thirty-minute flight on a small plane to Larsen Bay (which is often delayed by bad weather), then a skiff ride across Uyak. I always wish for a landing craft instead of an aluminum skiff when older relatives visit, struggling to hoist stiff legs over the high sides of the boat. Seeing their appreciation always renews my own gratitude for the beauty around us. Company is also a good excuse to pull out the kayaks or drop the crab pots. Misty and I went kayaking on a morning so calm that the loudest sounds were fin whales breathing and the splash of kittiwakes diving. Mostly we floated without paddling, watching harbor porpoises and seals surface around us.

One night before the moon was out we drifted in the skiff to see bioluminescence glimmering in the black water. We splashed the ocean over and over, sending trails of sparks shooting away from the paddle's slap. The skiff's wake swirled a glowing green path behind us. Wading into the water that night, each step of our boots was like kicking up stars.

As we close up the cabin, bears leave their tracks along the tide line flecked with the gold of the last cottonwood leaves. When Peter drains the water line he finds their wide prints in the trampled mud and water shooting up from bear bites in the pipe. Last winter our setnetter friends in neighboring Uganik Bay had a bear in their cabin. It climbed through a window and left through the wall. When we leave, we board up the doors and windows and hope we won't return to a mess of bear scat and chewed-up couches and mattresses. We also empty the pantry, which makes for interesting meals. For several days, we cook giant omelets to use up the eggs and garden onions.

I've heard subsistence described as "always getting ready," and it rings true with every seasonal transition in Alaska. I think of winterizing as always trying to guess what nature might destroy while we're away. Something will inevitably freeze or break, but we try to take things down that an earthquake could shake from the walls and store the solar panels and anything else the wind might take. I shouldn't admit it, but I find it almost as satisfying to put the garden beds to rest as it is to plant the first seeds in May. When I rake compost and seaweed over the cabbage leaves and broccoli stems, I imagine the soil resting under a layer of snow and it feels like making peace with the end of another season.

By November we've moved into the town of Kodiak. It's back to marking time with days of the week and dates on the calendar, back to telephones ringing, seatbelts, and grocery stores. In the winter, it's the small things that I'll miss from our season at the fishsite, like having time to write a real letter and starting the day with a slow walk in a quiet place.

the wait

TODAY MY SECOND SON is due. I'm just back from the playground where all the sunshine and the contentment of watching Liam conquering slides has me feeling like I don't need to give birth today. Labor should start in the refuge of night, with its empty roads and silent hospital hallways. That's how it was with our first baby. Or that was how it started: Liam wasn't born until after noon, but by then there was nothing real about the day outside. It was as if there had been no sunrise, no morning traffic, no kids racing out to recess.

When I was pregnant with Liam, I often woke in the night to roll over, heaving the hump of my belly with both hands, and found that my teeth had been traveling around in my mouth. I'd test my crooked bite, opening and shutting my jaw like a fish under a boot. Maybe I should have been reassured that my body was preparing for labor, but it was an odd feeling to have so little control. I couldn't even predict where my teeth would be in the morning. What I didn't know yet was how much control I would have to give up in the torrent of labor and birth and helpless new baby love.

Some nights just after he was born I lay awake and terrified thinking of how many ways there were to lose something so small. We start in such perfection. We can turn out so unpleasant. The night creaked with the ugliness of the world. Marching through the dark room were plagues and wars and all the mothers who have loved this fiercely and have still lost babies. When I shared my sleepless thoughts with Nathan, the friend who is also Liam's namesake—the terrible possibility that someone could just round us all up and put us in ovens, they had done it before, we are killing still—he offered this: "Try thinking about the culinary history of the world instead of the violent history, think of all the good food he has to look forward to, all of it cooked…in ovens!" It still makes me laugh, though I sometimes think back to the hormonal seismology of those first fragile days—the way women open for birth and push a life forward with such violence, it's as if every safe, comfortable place in a woman opens, and the force of it knocks something loose, and you can never shut out all the fear again.

෴

Waiting. I'm days overdue, just as I was with Liam. But this time I am not in a hurry. I will not eat hot peppers or have awkward sex with my husband to speed things along. My reluctance is not over the pain of pushing a baby into the world. That pain has a purpose and an ending. Although to be honest, it *is* different knowing what I'm waiting for this time around. Waves of pain and burning pushing, poop on the delivery table, blood and then more bleeding, breasts like cement bags and nipples strange as tide pool creatures.

The other day I had a meeting and didn't leave myself enough time for the leisurely walk I'd planned to get there. I raced out the door in a jacket that wouldn't zip over my round belly, past our neighbor's house—a woman in her eighties who spends much of her time in a pink bathrobe. I've seen her gravestone waiting for her at the cemetery; her husband is already there. Puffing past the fisherman's memorial, I thought for the first time about all the spaces they included for additional names. Remember making pictures on a Lite-Brite, the children's toy with rows of holes you filled with tiny colored pegs? The memorial looks like those empty pegs, except the holes are waiting for the engraved nameplates of each future fisherman lost at sea. That kind of waiting is sensible and rational, but it's something we avoid thinking about. Most people prefer the waiting that comes with a reward like dessert or retirement or Christmas.

Waiting to deliver, at least with this second baby, falls somewhere in between. I'd like to meet him, but I'm not quite ready for the pain. I'll be free of the internal weight, but my arms won't really be free again for years. Once he's born I'll be waiting for milk to come in and then for the swollen discomfort to pass, for stitches to heal, hemorrhoids to shrink, cramps to stop, cracked nipples to mend. Waiting to sit on wooden chairs again. To walk without shuffling. Waiting months for a full night of sleep.

I think my reluctance (which I'd rather think of as patience) over this due date is in facing twice the need. Another child needing to be fed, changed, comforted, held. Some nights, lying next to Liam and willing him to fall asleep, ideas for stories surface and slip away and I have nothing to write them on and as I try holding them in my memory and also try not to fall asleep, I wonder if giving as a mother makes me more or less myself.

◎◎

Luke was born early in the morning, sunny side up, which sounds much more pleasant than it actually was during labor. When it was time to push, he came so fast the doctor almost didn't catch him. When Luke was seven days old, I took him to the clinic for his checkup. Peter stayed home with Liam. In the doctor's office Luke wailed and peed like a sprinkler when I pulled off his diaper and then he pooped twice, and when the appointment was over I was sweating and shaky as I finally strapped his tiny body into the car seat and carried him to the car. I didn't cry. I am not as fragile this time around.

Mustard-colored baby poop was smeared across my fingers and wedding ring; I noticed it as I drove. At a stop sign near our house was a bare mountain ash with red berries so brilliant against the blue sky I had to pull off my sunglasses to see if it was a trick of the lens. My grandmother used to instruct my mom, "Make sure you remember this. Close your eyes and save this moment so you can always come back to it." I sat with the car idling at the stop sign, not waiting for traffic, just waiting long enough to be sure I saved this window full of clean sky, bright berries, the new baby sleeping beside me.

hunger & thirst

PETER SAYS, "The people on arctic expeditions who didn't get scurvy were the ones who ate maggots."

"I'd rather not eat maggots," I say. We'd been talking about life on Kodiak from the late 1700s to the mid-1800s, when the island was a Russian colony and scurvy was rampant among settlers, and about what we would do if Kodiak were suddenly cut off from the rest of the world, the way it was back then. For five years, between 1797 and 1802, no resupply ship reached the colony in Alaska. A string of Russian ships sank between Okhotsk and Alaska, each loss magnified by the effort of first hauling the cargo overland across Siberia to the coast. People in Alaska learned of shipwrecks when the flotsam and jetsam began washing onshore—a samovar, the stub of a large candle, bottles of sour wine, a straw hat from Hawaii, flagons of vodka, a ship's wheel.

"Or rose hips. You could gather them and eat them all winter," my husband says.

"That sounds better to me," I say. "I'm fine with eating rose hips."

"Dogs don't get scurvy. We could eat dogs," Pete says. "I'd eat Nettie before I'd eat Schooner."

"Peter!" Nettie is our new puppy. She's a bit of a handful.

The conversation started because I was surprised by all the mentions of hunger as I read about Kodiak under the rule of the Russian-American Company (RAC), the sea otter hunting company that Grigorii Shelikov began here in 1784. I knew of hardships imposed on the island's Alutiiq people—forced labor and introduced diseases and outright violence. But I didn't expect quite so many references to starvation. The abundance of seafood is a big reason we live here. After Peter took the MCAT, he had to decide whether to give up salmon fishing for medical school. He chose fishing for the free time in winter and the potential of lucrative seasons, but also because he likes harvesting a healthy, sustainable food. We eat frozen salmon, halibut, crab, and cod all winter. By June we've tried every possible seafood recipe and spice rub, and another frozen fillet is the last thing we're in the mood for, and then we grill the first fresh salmon of the summer and agree that there is nothing better.

When Pavel Golovin visited Kodiak in 1861, he wrote about eating enormous crabs with legs the length of a man's arm. "Yesterday at supper five of us could not finish the legs of one crab!"

For thousands of years before Europeans arrived, the Kodiak Archipelago sustained the Alutiiq people, at one time supporting a population in the tens of thousands. As well as fishing and harvesting shellfish and plants, the people of Kodiak hunted marine mammals with a mastery the Russians quickly recognized and exploited. Still, there were months of hunger. Gavril Davydov, a Russian sailor in Kodiak in 1802, noted that early spring was the leanest time of the year, when "the islanders are short of food supplies and eat only shellfish or pieces of the remaining *iukola* (dried fish)—which, however, few have left." Even the ten missionaries from the Valaam Monastery who arrived at Kodiak in the fall of 1794 had to fend for themselves. Father Iosaph wrote, "Starvation has stalked this place ever since our arrival. We cleaned out rotten dried salmon three years old to have enough to eat." When the RAC imposed year-round sea otter hunting, Alutiiq family units were broken and the subsistence harvest cycle disrupted, aggravating seasonal food shortages and causing starvation in winter months.

"We didn't go hungry; we ate snails," Peter says. He's still thinking about how we would survive if the container ships that deliver up to forty-two thousand pounds of groceries to Kodiak each week didn't arrive. He ate snails last January, during a fishing trip for tanner crab along the east side of Kodiak. They'd eaten all the meat on board the boat, so when they hauled up crab pots with sea snails attached, Peter boiled them for dinner, and later made snail chowder, and then snail fritters.

Peter is an adventurous eater. On our honeymoon he ate an apple-sized fried spider in Laos, and he's been known to eat roadkill—like a goanna lizard in Australia. His enthusiasm makes me think of Martin Sauer trying local fare on a visit to Kodiak in 1790. "I had a young sea otter dressed, and it tasted exactly like suckling pig," Sauer wrote. Of sea lion, "I thought it bad and filthy; but the head, which is equal in size to that of a large ox, I thought very good, if well-stewed, and eaten with farina and other edible roots." Sauer found halibut dry but liked the fins and tail. Peter feels the same way.

Captain Yuri Lisianski, who wintered in the Russian colony in 1804, ate crow, fricasseed. "Though not very delicate, it was a considerable relief to the perpetual uniformity of salt meat, and proved as healthful as any provision we could be supplied with," he wrote.

Maybe we wouldn't die of scurvy today, but when I try to imagine living here two hundred years ago, I think I understand why food was frequently mentioned in journals and letters. For the months it took to reach the colony, people subsisted mainly on hardtack and dried meat. Once in Alaska, there was little dietary variety, and settlers felt the lack of staples they'd been accustomed to—tea and flour were now luxuries.

"Through necessity they scorned nothing: they ate eagles, crows, cuttlefish, and, in general, anything they could find. Only those afflicted with scurvy, which was endemic in the settlement, were given millet with molasses and beer brewed from fir cones," wrote historian P. A. Tikhmenev.

How welcome the chocolate and wine must have been from Gonzalo Lopez de Haro, Spanish captain of the *San Carlos*, when he visited the Russian settlement at Three Saints Bay on Kodiak in 1788. De Haro wrote, "I being desirous of Acquiring all the Information possible for the Success of the

Expedition so important to our Sovereign, took occasion to give him [Delarov, the manager of the settlement] a present of a Cask of Wine, Chocolate, and other things, to see if by this means might be achieved the most important purpose of this Expedition. He appeared very grateful, and soon began to speak more substantially and more plainly."

I'm pretty sure that if I were wintering on a remote island, eating mainly whale and cod, I'd give up all my secrets in exchange for wine and chocolate.

Russian colonists tried to grow food on Kodiak—they planted kitchen gardens of carrots, turnips, potatoes, and radishes, but rye and wheat wouldn't mature and most crops didn't thrive. There's a reason hoop houses and greenhouses are hugely popular here, otherwise most vegetables don't ripen before summer ends. F. P. Wrangell, chief manager of Russian America in the 1830s, wrote that potatoes were grown "more as a delicacy for a few days in the autumn than a source of food through the year." Wild goats wouldn't breed, and bears ate imported cattle.

K. T. Khlebnikov described one of Baranov's trips around Kodiak Island: "It could have been considered quite ordinary and normal if on the journey there had been peaceful shelter and warm food, but . . . often they were hungry and cold, and had to consume shellfish they gathered from the beach at low tide. Among these there would often be poisonous ones, and instead of the joys of slaking one's hunger there would be cramps and convulsions and the death which usually followed would itself be accounted a joyous release."

Baranov once lost 140 Kodiak hunters to paralytic shellfish poisoning when the men ate contaminated mussels near Sitka. It must have been a horrific scene, that many men dying at the same time, paralyzed and suffocating along the beach.

We don't eat Kodiak mussels, knowing that a blue mussel can become toxic with PSP in less than an hour. One death here in 1993 was attributed to eating mussels with 19,600 mg of saxitoxin. With that concentration, eating a single mussel could kill you. We don't go clamming either, although people do, in spite of PSP poisonings here every few years. We have the luxury of such choices because we have enough to eat.

Before we had kids, Peter and I traveled through India—where beauty and ugliness seemed equally, continuously present, right up until the sun set thick in a red sky and streets gathered rows of sleeping bodies—and I realized that the personality I give myself credit for, my kindness or generosity, is the privilege of my country of birth. I swore I would never take the ease of my life for granted again. And for at least a month, I savored the cold, clean air and wild, empty space that is Alaska. It didn't take very long for my good intentions to fade. But sometimes reading history, I get a glimpse of my good luck to live here and now.

The Russian settlements were in desperate need of food during the winter of 1805–1806 when Count Nikolai Rezanov, a major shareholder of the RAC, traveled around the colonies. Rezanov mustered the least scurvy-afflicted men in Sitka and sailed south. As they waited in California for supplies, Rezanov wrote, "The abundance of breadstuffs there as compared to our lack of them, and the prospect of facing starvation again in the future were hourly subject of conversation among our men. We noticed their inclination and desire to remain permanently and took measure against their desertion."

Can you blame them?

Working as a sailor or low-level employee of the RAC was a pretty bad deal. Sailors weakened by scurvy were generally left at any outpost that had healthier men who could take their place. Boats were rudimentary and prone to sinking. Davydov wrote that most ships coming from Okhotsk were built and manned "in complete ignorance of the rules for doing these things ... carried out under the very crudest of conditions and with crude equipment." Even on land, living quarters were usually cramped and dirty, and low-level RAC employees were often in debt to the company and denied the same food and goods that higher officials had access to. Many Russian settlers arrived in Alaska already suffering from "alcoholism, tuberculosis, syphilis, gonorrhea, and nutritional diseases," wrote Robert Fortuine in *Chills and Fever*, noting that there was almost no medical care in the colony. Occasionally ship's doctors passed through, like the surgeon Karl Mordgorst who spent a winter in Kodiak in 1807, ineptly amputating both feet and a few fingers of a Scottish sailor before leaving for Russia.

Life in Russian America sometimes reads like a reality television formula—force strong personalities together in a challenging environment and give them booze. With a time machine, I could gather up a cast for a riveting show: There's Alexander Baranov—an adulterer who was short and stocky and fond of an ill-fitting black wig. "He had no love of fashion, and preferred the uniform he had worn when promoted [1805] to anything new, regardless of the fact that in 14 years, changing fashions had made it outmoded," noted K. T. Khlebnikov in his biography. Baranov, the chief manager from 1790 to 1818, asked repeatedly to be relieved of his post. Twice, men hired as his replacement died en route, and eventually, Baranov resigned himself to Alaska, dying on the way back to Russia at the age of seventy-two, by then "decrepit in body and depressed in spirit," wrote historian C. L. Andrews.

And there's Baranov's Kodiak mistress, Anna, a woman who had affairs of her own, who walked "straightly and proudly, dressed in red silk kerchief and close-fitting woolen dress that showed her firm breasts." At least that's how biographer Hector Chevigny describes her. But then Chevigny mentions firm breasts almost every time he writes about a woman, which makes me a little suspicious of his descriptive accuracy.

There's Nikolai Rezanov, famous for his love affair with Concepcion Arguello, the fifteen-year-old daughter of a Spanish commandant in California. The smitten Georg von Langsdorff, Rezanov's doctor, wrote journal entries about Concepcion's beautiful teeth, cheerfulness, and "love-inspiring" eyes, as well as "her shapeliness of figure" and "a thousand other charms." Some authors claim that Rezanov killed himself galloping ardently across Russia to obtain permission for the marriage, while others believe he was just trying to arrive before news that he'd secretly ordered an attack against Japan. Concepcion became a nun.

And there are Baranov's drinking buddies, including American captain and fur trader John D'Wolf, husband of Mary Melville. Mary was Herman Melville's aunt, and D'Wolf is thought to have sparked the writer's interest in the sea.

Also, the inseparable Nikolai Khvostov and Gavril Davydov, who died together in *Thelma and Louise* fashion. Baranov often entertained the pair in Kodiak, though he sometimes had to lock himself in at night because Khvostov would shoot out windows when he was drunk. Davydov liked to read, explore, and write down his observations, whereas Khvostov, according to Rezanov, "did nothing but drink and rampage." Of the several versions of their last night in St. Petersburg in October 1809, the one I prefer tells of Khvostov and Davydov heading home after drinking with old friends from the colony. When they tried to leap together from a raised drawbridge onto a passing ship, they hit the sails and were thrown into the Neva River and drowned.

Reading about Russian America, I'm drawn to the narratives of friendship and conflict and love affairs, the drinking and eating, the daily. It makes history tangible to recognize a shared experience of place. I like finding my love for this island echoed back from hundreds of years ago. When Gavril Davydov hiked up a mountain behind Kodiak in the spring of 1803, he wrote, "I stood with great pleasure in the same spot for more than half an hour admiring this magnificent sight.... A man becomes more content with his existence when he is standing on a high mountain breathing the excellent pure air.... He looks at the unencompassable width of the ocean and dreams of his enterprise, brings himself close to the whole world and to those distant lands that he has left behind." I've hiked to the same views and felt the same lifted spirits.

On other days, when gales topple spruce trees onto roofs or sink fishing boats, when summer fog grounds flights for days, I think of Pavel Golovin describing the colony as a place "where nature itself has placed limits on the well-being of men" or of Baranov claiming that he hosted dances "to bring an end to the rain."

Today in every bar there's a bell with a well-worn line. Fishermen ring it—back from weeks or months on the boat, for the sake of instant friendship or to show off a good season by buying a round for everyone in the bar—and our bars are seldom empty. Drinking has been a part of Kodiak history since the days of the Russian-American Company. Bars boomed during the heyday of crab and shrimp fishing, days of burlesque dancers and topless waitresses, at least until the fisheries crashed. After the 1964 tsunami, downtown bars were some of the first businesses to reopen, though the buildings that held them were little more than plywood shacks.

Even during Prohibition in the 1920s, Harold Phelps, a radio station employee, remarked, "The only crops around Kodiak were salmon, halibut, herring, blue foxes, and moonshine."

Frederick Sargent was sent to Kodiak to inventory the holdings of the Russian-American Company after the sale of Alaska. On May 31, 1869, his diary reads simply, "The town is drunk."

When Rezanov stopped in Kodiak in 1805, he called it "a drunken republic." Though the sale of liquor was forbidden in the later years of the Russian-American colonies, people made their own homebrew called *kvass* with cranberries or roots. Krusenstern, the captain of Rezanov's ship, wrote that company employees in Kodiak suffered from a lack of food similar to those at sea and that "the only item of which there is no scarcity is vodka."

Russian colonists may have been hard drinkers when they arrived here, but long, dark, uncomfortable winters probably didn't help their habits. While Baranov was manager of the colony, he seems to have reinterpreted Shelikov's instructions to the first RAC manager, Evstratii Ivanovich Delarov—"Do not let men get drunk under any circumstances"—as something more like, "some men may get drunk for a variety of circumstances." One such circumstance was in 1809, when Baranov used alcohol to foil an assassination attempt. After learning that several men were plotting to kill him and take charge of the fort in Sitka, Baranov asked an employee to "ply them with vodka," and then broke into the room and ordered the mutineers thrown in irons, wrote K. T. Klebnikov.

Baranov had few chances to show munificence. Treating his employees to drinks was likely the only time Baranov felt more camaraderie than animosity from his men. To celebrate the christening of the first ship built in the colony, Baranov made two buckets of vodka to share. Some biographers speculate that those "buckets" were actually tierces—thousand-pound containers used to cure king salmon—because Baranov noted that the second bucket held 216 pounds of the company's flour.

Baranov was aware of his many detractors—the clergy, his employees, even men who had never met him, including the writer Washington Irving, who described Baranov's entertaining style: "If you do not drink raw rum and boiling punch as strong as sulfur he will insult you as soon as he gets drunk, which will be very shortly after sitting down to table."

Baranov defended himself in a letter to Shelikov. "It is not true that we drink vodka all the time. Nobody with the exception of myself and Izmailov makes it, or at least if the hunters make it too, it is done in such secrecy that I never hear of it. But when I make it I do so only once or twice a year, first, when I return from a tour of inspection or a journey and find a barrel or two of raspberry and bilberry juice prepared for the occasion, and second, on my birthday, I make a bucket of vodka and treat everybody to it. Sometimes on Christmas and Easter I make some out of makaracha roots, half a bucket, and this is all."

Some historians believe that Baranov suffered physical pains from the cold climate of Alaska, while others suggest he was an alcoholic. Robert Fortuine wrote that Baranov "seemed to get some relief, or at least a measure of oblivion, from alcohol." Perhaps Baranov drank to ease the pressure of a position he no longer wanted and couldn't get free of, or to numb his fatigue and his isolation in this remote place. In Kodiak's bars, the same desires—for relief or oblivion, for sex or conversation or shelter from a raw day—are still drowned nightly in round after round.

In the end, maintaining a remote colony in Alaska proved too difficult. After 150 years the Russian-American Company faded away, leaving sea otter populations nearly extinct and Alutiiq culture inalterably changed. Russian names remain on boats and parks and landmarks around Kodiak. We are living among the ghosts of the RAC—their bloodlines, surnames, Russian Orthodox religion, and the heavy drinking that fishermen have since claimed as their legacy. We're busy repeating their stories in varying degrees, falling in love, thinking of our next meal, wondering when the rain will end. So busy we hardly think of them at all, even as we live on streets bearing their names.

homing

THERE ARE THINGS I forgot about Kodiak in the dozen years between high school graduation and our move back to the island. For instance, how it feels to fly home to Kodiak, an hour trip from Anchorage, only to circle town several times—"I can see my house!"—and then turn back to the mainland because the pilot decided it was just too windy or foggy to make the approach. For the next hour you are thinking of nothing but finding a place to sleep, missing work the following day, rescheduling your flight, loading the kids into a motel van.

And I forgot that there are days you can't actually walk here. We wake to fluffy new snow, but it's a bruising snowball consistency by lunch and then turns to rain, filling a citywide puddle over the ice. To cross parking lots you scoot a few inches at a time without lifting your feet, preferably clutching the sides of cars or buildings. By the end of winter, melting snow banks reveal solitary ice cleats all over town.

During one storm this winter, I drove past a giant inflatable snowman somersaulting down the bike path as the radio DJ urged fishermen to get down to the harbors to check on their boats. Blowing snow blurred the mountain edges, and williwaws streaked down the channel. The storm uprooted dozens of spruce trees that vanished within days to folks eager for free firewood, the sound of wind replaced by the sound of chainsaws. Our New Year's Eve fireworks this year were last summer's Fourth of July display that was cancelled because of bad weather.

We've just had a week of clear skies, but we haven't had a chance to enjoy it. Pete and I bought our first house this year, and we've been busy painting, stripping wallpaper, and taking power tools away from our toddler. I've spent far too much time trying to choose between shades of white paint—Petticoat White, Swan White, Wedding White, Journal White. We finally settled on Swiss Coffee, a name that implies that in Switzerland, people don't take coffee in their milk.

On a recent Saturday morning we decided to leave the boxes and projects behind. We loaded Liam, the dogs, and a thermos of coffee into the truck and headed to Narrow Cape. On these winter days of afternoon sunsets when the light always slips away too early, it felt good to be out and waiting for the sun to rise. It was just getting light when we stopped to see the eagles crouched around the last silver salmon in the creek. At Narrow Cape, we stopped again for the ranch buffalo that had formed an indifferent roadblock.

Years ago, I often made this drive with my family. We sometimes fished or picked salmonberries or looked for fossils at Narrow Cape, but Boat Bay was our favorite picnic spot. When I was fourteen I found a faded rubber duck on this beach. Years later in a college oceanography class I learned it was from a famous container ship spill that sent thousands of plastic bath toys overboard during a storm. The toys washed up all over the Pacific, helping oceanologists track and study ocean currents. A while ago I pulled the duck from my childhood trunk and added it to Liam's bathtub toys. During baths it bobs around the islands of his knees, a small herald of the circular nature of currents and life.

Now they've paved the road as far as the rocket launch site, and there are enormous houses in Pasagshak, where there used to be just one-room cabins. Pasagshak felt much farther away when I was a kid. That's the thing about moving back to the town you grew up in. Every place you go holds stories, new memories are layered over the old.

It makes me envy friends who have come here from other places, who fell in love with Kodiak and decided to stay. Memory adds a wistful significance to sounds and smells and certain slants of light. Golden crown sparrows will always sing of summers home from college, the taste of canned beer, and kissing and bonfires. It's surprising sometimes to notice that we are growing older in this place where for so long we were young.

We parked by a frozen creek and watched as three surfers in hooded wetsuits rode waves that shifted from green to white. Then the beach was empty and the dogs looped across the sand. Boat Bay is different from the rocky beaches around town. Instead of a dark wall of spruce trees framing the view, there are grassy bluffs that roll toward the mountains. This beach makes the best sounds. On stormy days, the waves thunder and fling driftwood the size of sea lions up into the creek beds between the bluffs. Today the curl and trip of water is steady and soothing. On the drive home I collect a new list of colors—White Snow on Alder Branches, Sunshine White behind Winter Clouds, the Bone White Peaks of Kodiak Island.

a lake by any other name

To Harold —
I still think Fort
Greeley men are "tops"!
Love Rose

LAKE ROSE TEED is not an ordinary lake. A causeway passes through the tip of its hourglass shape, cutting the reflected image of mountains in two. The water is nearly level with the road, and in the fall spawning salmon rise like red waves. In 1964 when the Good Friday earthquake dropped the lake 1.7 meters, tidal salt water flowed in, and soon the coho salmon population surged from hundreds to thousands. Culverts along the road allow salmon through the causeway to spawn and feed and follow Pasagshak River out to sea. The water is a mirror of the sky or a window down to salmon and smelt, Dolly Vardens, sculpins, and starry flounders.

Where small spawning streams enter the northern tip of the lake— contained and still under a ring of mountains—you feel far from the sound of waves and river, while the other side of Lake Rose Teed winds and rolls and rushes into the bay. As a girl, I thought Rose Teed was the name of a local wildflower until I learned the lake was named for a pretty young woman who charmed soldiers in Kodiak during World War II.

Rose Teed was not an ordinary girl. She was an extraordinary beauty with a face made for black-and-white photographs and voluptuous curves that inspired army engineers in Kodiak when they surveyed a lake with an "hourglass figure." Her beauty was her ticket out of an imperfect childhood. After modeling as a teenager in Chicago, she won a beauty contest that led to a screen test with Warner Brothers in Hollywood. She danced on Broadway. She married well, as they say. And her name remains on a lovely lake in Alaska.

I was drawn to Rose because I recognized something, some hunger that beauty breeds. A pretty girl feels entitled to adoration. She wants the world to love her. I was sixteen when I worked at a coffee shop across from the boat harbor in Kodiak. I watched the names of wives and daughters slip by from harbor to fishing grounds, names as familiar as streets. I thought that a boat named for a wife was about the most romantic tribute there was. I didn't think of dead fish or drowned fishermen; I liked the idea of carrying a woman's name through distance and absence.

Unlikely as it was for a daughter of teachers, I wanted to be the namesake of a fishing boat. And though I didn't want to marry a fisherman who would be gone for months at a time, I daydreamed of the boat, some sleek highliner gliding past town. The *Sara C.* It even sounded right. Spoken, it would sound like the *Sara Sea*. I imagined my name on the hull, proof I was beloved.

Poems and twenties stuffed into the coffee shop tip jar were my first notion of what beauty might bring you. How any pretty girl can be enough to spark the imagination, to attach attributes, to create an ideal from an unknown.

At first I couldn't find her. More than a million people volunteered for the USO from 1941 to 1947. There were more than four hundred thousand performances for the GIs of World War II; maybe Rose wasn't particularly well known.

Then I found her obituary in the *New York Times*. Rose Cecelia Teed Wohlstetter died in May 2006, at the age of eighty-four. But I was looking for "the sweetheart of Kodiak Island," the girl *Life Magazine* "presented" to GIs on Kodiak with a full-page layout of pictures engraved on copper. The *Kodiak Bear* newspaper ran a double press so that "everybody could send one copy home and pin the other up in his dugout or barracks." The *Kodiak Bear* called them "the finest art layout in the history of military journalism."

To the men stationed here, Kodiak Island must have seemed as remote as any base in the South Pacific. Year-round gales, fog, and rain made the island feel even more desolate. Servicemen grumbled about boredom, bad weather, and the price of whiskey—twenty-two dollars a pint—in their journals and in letters home.

"Dear Mary: Well, well. I have seen Kodiak," wrote George K. Brodie, stationed at the naval base here in 1938. "The streets are mud and dirt and snow and puddles with 'sparrow lunches' laying here and there. There is no street lighting system and no sidewalks. There are not even any definitely layed out streets as far as block and house numbers are concerned. About three licker [*sic*] stores. Right now there is *nothing* at *all* pretty, romantic, unique, cute or quant [*sic*] about any of it."

There were few single girls in Kodiak, a town with only a few hundred people. For company, men wallpapered their barracks with pinups. It was the era of pinup art—"posters representing every man's dream of the perfect woman," according to *Life Magazine*—and "cheesecake photos" of scantily clothed ladies provocatively posed to accentuate their curves and legs. During the 1940s, such pictures were everywhere, from Vargas girls painted on tanks and airplanes to posters and playing cards mass-produced for troop morale. I'd like to think those old photos were more innocent than the nude pinups in magazines today. They were at least truer to the girl; the old pinups weren't airbrushed into being indistinguishable. I'm thinking of Betty Grable's famous pose, smiling over her shoulder, the way her appeal was as much her familiarity as it was her perfect "gams." Or maybe these women came to seem like the possibility of making it home again, having a future, a family, being loved, being alive.

Imagine the daydreams these pinups inspired. And then imagine a photo peeling itself right off that cold, cement wall and standing within reach, wearing a sparkly little number and kicking those endless legs up, north to Alaska! A real woman, speaking and moving before your eyes. To meet Rose in person and to have her pictures from *Life Magazine*—it would have been like confirmation that pinup girls could materialize, and if that was possible, then maybe if you dreamed it enough, the girl of your dreams might even, someday, be your wife.

　　　◎◎

It's hard to imagine it now, but Kodiak felt dangerously close to the war. On June 3, 1942, just two days after Al Jolson and comedian Joe E. Brown performed here on their USO tour in Alaska, with Rose along as a chorine dancer, Japanese carrier-based bombers and fighters killed fifty-two U.S. personnel at Fort Mears and Dutch Harbor, six hundred miles from Kodiak Island.

Military dependents had been evacuated from Kodiak in December. During that winter, blackouts were enforced with patrols to ensure that no lantern lights, headlights, or cigarettes gave the town away. Many families had dug trenches near their homes, and there was a false town set up at Holiday Beach to deter Japanese bombers.

Downtown Kodiak was a few rows of squat wooden buildings along the water, with dirt streets that turned to mud when it rained and boardwalks rather than sidewalks. The two bars in town closed by 9:00 p.m. to discourage soldiers from becoming disorderly, but there were bars outside of town that served till morning and a red-light district known as "the Hill," where customers lined up on paydays, wrote Joseph Driscoll in *War Discovers Alaska*. Mornings after busloads of sailors and soldiers went drinking in Kodiak, local children would hunt through the mud outside of the bars for coins and wristwatches.

Rose performed for packed houses at both the navy and army clubs in Kodiak. USO Camp Shows were generally standing room only. The Kodiak newspaper declared, "We have turned down flattering offers from all sorts of movie queens to be our girl. We are a loyal bunch up here and we've given our heart to Rose and that's all there is to it."

I'd like to ask a man in the audience that night, "What made Rose extraordinary?" Those men, if they're still alive, are in their nineties. My chances of finding one who could share that memory are waning. Visitors to the World War II museum in Kodiak are usually the grown children of those men, searching for more of their fathers.

When I imagine Rose in Kodiak, I can't help thinking of the things I did at twenty, home from college for the summer, restless in the endless June light. I picture a group of tipsy chorus girls running down a soft mossy hill near Miller Point. They laugh and shriek, pulling off shoes and clothes at the edge of the lake before slipping into the dark water. The boy they brought along is in love with every one of these young glowing girls shining under a summer moon. But that is my own story. Rose was not a small-town girl. Her appeal may very well have been in her glamour, in the big-city way she shrugged off her fur coat at the bar, held a cigarette, ordered a drink. She was blazing with ambition. She was a girl who was going places.

Rose played an American showgirl in the musical *High Kickers* in New York. Television star Milton Berle mentioned her as a "gorgeous showgirl" in his autobiography, and George Jessel, an actor and entertainer, listed Rose among his "favorite ladies" in his autobiography. As a teenager, she was featured in the *Chicago Herald-American* story "Chicago's Typical Daughters," which followed Rose and another beauty contestant to Hollywood. The reporter described the girls as "wide-eyed and breathless, knowing this is the land where anything can happen—because they themselves are young and beautiful."

In the article, Rose said, "Nothing is going to stop me. Even if I don't get a contract this time, I will later. I've made up my mind that I'll reach the top—no matter how long it takes and how hard the climbing may be." Her screen test didn't lead to an offer, but eventually Rose landed a part as a dancer in *The Ziegfeld Follies* (think rhinestones, top hats, peacock-sized headdresses, lavish costumes and sets).

"Fort Greely's Rose Teed... the girl for whom one of our loveliest lakes has been named is now a 'Follies Girl'... which is just about the nicest thing that can happen to a girl in the show business," reported the *Kodiak Bear* newspaper. "It means that she has been selected as one of the world's most beautiful girls, and boy are we proud of our gal!"

Rose sent a letter to Kodiak in 1943, writing:

Dear Friends at Kodiak,

Happy New Year to you! I have some nice news for you. I've made the Ziegfeld Follies and I'm right in the midst of rehearsal and that's why I haven't written you sooner.

Believe me we have been rehearsing for almost three weeks—day and night, so I don't have much time for myself. The show opens in Boston about the Fifteenth of January. So now I'm a "Follies Girl" and it's fun. I am at long last sending you a picture for the Kodiak Bear office and also for the paper. It's been a long time coming but I know you'll forgive the delay.

I can't tell you how thrilled I am about my lake, and believe me it's been wonderful publicity for me so if I ever get anywhere you fellows can take the credit for it. It certainly has been swell for me and I appreciate it very much . . .

Well, this is just a short note of hello and I wish all of you a happy new year and to let you know I am thinking that my Fort Greely fellows are tops! I really mean that and I boast about all of you and about our paper. It's wonderful to feel I sort of belong to you and you all sort of belong to me—I guess you know what I mean.

Rose married Charles Wohlstetter in 1944. The war ended; men returned to real women or didn't return at all. Kodiak's Fort Greely was closed, leaving relics like crumbling bunkers and Lake Rose Teed. Rose had three sons. She didn't return to Broadway for thirty years. She never saw the lake on Kodiak. Today, few people in town know anything about her.

＠＠

At the start of my search for the namesake of Lake Rose Teed, I was elated to find any hint of Rose, even phrases like *unusual Eustachian Valve Function*, which are linked to her married name, Wohlstetter. That's because the New York University Non-Invasive Cardiology Laboratory is named for Rose and her husband. I'd rather people hear my name and think of white swans on a peaceful lake, but I'd settle for a life-saving medical facility.

Her married life sounded charmed. A summerhouse on Long Island and a Park Avenue apartment decorated with sculptures by Giacometti and Degas and paintings by Matisse and Pissarro. Charles and Rose flew to California to dance and drink at the Palm Springs Racquet Club, which they co-owned. They bought Château Bouscaut, a winery in France, where they played cards and tennis with diplomats. Rose was twenty-two when she married Charles Wohlstetter, thirty-four, a Wall Street broker and entrepreneur who had always liked showgirls. He liked making money and spending it. A 1969 article in *Business Week* described him as a man who "wears his money in fine style. He drives about town on weekends in an espresso-colored Rolls-Royce." By the time he sold his phone business, it had $6 billion in assets, $3 billion in annual revenues, and operated in thirty-two states, South America, Asia, Europe, and the Middle East.

I read all this in Charles Wohlstetter's memoir, *The Right Time, the Right Place*, a book bulky with names—Carl Sandburg, Dorothy Parker, Milton Berle, George Gershwin, Billy Rose, Marlene Dietrich, Salvador Dalí. Rose, it turns out, met Salvador Dalí as she was lying on a massage table at Billy Rose's mansion. That was one of the few stories about her. I had hoped that Charles's life story might show me Rose as a wife and mother. Yet reading it, I felt I lost her.

When her sons asked Rose about her early years, she gave clipped or one-word answers. Her sons didn't know that Rose was once "the sweetheart of Kodiak." Did Rose see giving up her youthful ambitions as a relief or a loss? Was marriage her lucky break? Rose, a girl with a high school education, lived her final years in a Park Avenue apartment with eleven bedrooms and three staff rooms. The apartment later sold for more than $10 million, according to the *New York Observer*.

As Rose was dying, her sons found scrapbooks at the bottom of her closet. The brothers stood around the dining room table, looking through old modeling photos and clips about her performances that they'd never seen before—Rose smiling on the gangplank of an ocean liner, or walking through a snowstorm in a bathing suit, or wearing a raccoon coat at a college football game with a hotdog in her white gloved hand. In one of the old scrapbooks there is a photo of Rose Teed standing with a bouquet in the doorway of the *Super Chief,* setting off for her screen test in Hollywood. The caption reads, "Happiness, comfort, and possibly fame and fortune are ahead."

Her son Philip wrote about her youthful ambitions in her eulogy: "And the truth is, Rose, you did reach the top, and for you, it was us, your kids, nothing made you glow more." I want to believe that. Because I am steeped in the work of these years of raising children and navigating a marriage and I am wondering who I will emerge as, what I will sacrifice—I want Rose to tell me that those were the best years, they were enough.

A tundra swan is moving across Lake Rose Teed, over a mirror of mountains. Below the swan, fish are feeding or leaving, returning and dying. The scent of streams that pulls fish from the bay is stronger than cottonwoods. The scent lures them in spite of the river's resistance, in spite of the road dividing the lake. The scent pulls them into a place of stillness. The lake remains, the truest beauty in this story.

elementary love

Ms. Stevens,

You asked me in your substitute teacher plans to leave a note about how your second graders behaved today.

Well, the kids came in pretty wound up after recess. Apparently there was a lot of kissing on the playground. What can you do? It's springtime. Unfortunately not springtimey enough for the dress I chose to wear this morning, in which I froze during recess duty as I stood counting down the minutes until I could blow the whistle and get back inside.

When the phone rang this morning and I agreed to take your class, I grabbed this dress because there wasn't enough time to iron something *and* pack a lunch—and lunch is a substitute teacher's only comfort. Why did I answer the phone? I can never invent an excuse under pressure. I'm not even sure why I'm substitute teaching this year when I'm trying to get through a master's program and the whole reason for going back to school was to avoid teaching elementary school again.

Back to our day. Your lesson plans told me to remind the second graders during writing time that good writers write what they know. Really? What exactly does a seven-year-old know? They know who Caitlin kissed on the playground during recess and why. She kissed him because he had her trapped and she needed to get away. No, she kissed him because she didn't like him. No, that was another boy. It sounds like Caitlin kisses a lot of boys.

FYI, most of the kids didn't even get two sentences written down. Maybe they'd do better writing fiction. Or maybe an essay on why it's cruel to name your kids weird things. You have a kid named Ocean *and* a kid named Rice? A teacher told me during recess that Ocean has a sister named Lake and a brother named River. "No way," I said. "It's true," she said. "We have a running bet as to what number four will be named." Rice walked by me in the classroom this afternoon muttering, "Why did they have to name me Rice? It's so STUPID." I bet he thinks that every day of his life until he's old enough to legally change it.

Your lesson plans made me think of some other writing advice. *Forget about writing. Put down anything. Write honestly. Just scribble, scribble, scribble.* Frank McCourt said that. When you were in the second grade, Ms. Stevens, you were quite chubby. I remember because your older brother was the first boy I ever loved, the first boy I ever kissed, actually. He was lanky and blond and blue-eyed. When we were fifth graders, he ran up to me on the playground and kissed me on the cheek. And we kissed again when we were sixteen, standing on his front porch. I'd loved him for years by then, but I had braces and no idea what to do so I pulled away and gave him an awkward hug and I knew it was the wrong response. It wasn't long before he broke my heart for a girl who knew how to do more than hug.

She's back in town working at the coffee shop. She was a born-again Christian for a while, but she seems to be unborn again now. I can't remember if she was working when I saw you at that same coffee shop the other day on a date with a kid I recognize from high school. I think he was a wrestler. Your divorce must have gone through. I can't remember who told me about your divorce. This is a small town.

It isn't knowing everyone and everyone's business that makes the town feel small. It's driving back and forth on the same streets we drove in high school, back and forth, for hours, singing along to a mixed tape and hoping to pass the trucks of certain boys, hungry for something, anything, to happen. It's driving those same streets in a station wagon that smells like crackers and wet dog, wondering where that hunger went and when we started switching the radio off to drive because it's quiet we long for now.

There's a teacher down the hall whose wife had an affair and left him. He went to high school with us too. A friend of mine told me that the same day she heard they'd separated, she saw him buying condoms at the grocery store and then saw him out at the bar that night. I wish she hadn't told me, not because I think of it when I see him, though I do, but because I already feel self-conscious buying wine on a weeknight. I wonder what things have been noted—my buying pregnancy tests before I was married, mornings my car was still parked downtown.

Today I found myself walking back and forth past your bulletin board to steal a look at the photos of your brother and his newborn baby and his wife, a French Canadian. I was trying to decide if I'm prettier than her. I wonder if she speaks French to the baby, if her lullabies sound sweeter. I wish I spoke French.

I see that you've marked the last day of the school year with a big heart and a smiley face. I think you've been counting down the days for quite a while. The kids love you, but I'm not sure you love them in quite the same way. Although that day I stood waiting for my coffee next to you and your date I could hear you talking all about them. I remember thinking, thank God I'm done with dating.

Being in your classroom all I can think is, thank God I'm done with teaching. But if this were my classroom it would be a whole lot cleaner. True, it's the end of the school year, but this classroom was kind of messy when I subbed in here last fall. There's an envelope from a school district in Hawaii on top of the pile of papers covering your desk. I'm pretty sure they pay teachers nothing in Hawaii. But I have definitely daydreamed my way through a staff meeting or two, imagining a beach at the end of the school day.

I think I'll make another lap past the bulletin board. I've only seen your brother once in the past few years. We were at Walmart. It made me feel old and lame to see him there, to talk over blue shopping carts. I dreamed about him for days. Once I climbed up to his window during high school. He wasn't home and then I sort of fell out of the window in slow motion. I was lucky I didn't break an arm or a leg. I'd been drinking. I was lucky I didn't get caught. My parents would have been ashamed. I was an honor student from a nice family.

There was one day that same year when I left school between classes. I was so tired of being good, tired of hiding sadness. Weary with depression—a word I didn't recognize or claim. Maybe I never would have been brave enough to cut through the skin. But it was like another girl was sleepwalking in my place. I watched her movements with a calm detachment. She was done. Except the phone rang in the middle of the afternoon and it was your brother and he said he was calling for no real reason. We hadn't talked for months. I don't know if he called from a pay phone or from the school office or how he knew I was home. I don't even remember what he said, just that it mattered that someone had thought of me right at that moment. The timing of that phone call was probably happenstance, but it felt like a small miracle. I would never tell anyone this, but it made me believe in that saying, *God acts in mysterious ways*. As if God himself said, *Stick around kid or you'll miss out on all the good stuff*. It made me think that our connections to other people might serve some purpose without our even knowing it.

The kids have gone home. I'm just sitting here at your desk, scribbling.

pacific sandwiches

A DISPROPORTIONATELY large number of tourists travel from Kodiak to that other Pacific archipelago, the Hawaiian Islands, every year. As early as 1816, naturalist Adelbert von Chamissos mentioned in his journal, "I have even encountered dislodged Kadiakans in the Sandwich Islands." Everyone here can think of some neighbor who finally up and moved there permanently. They say Hawaiians have two seasons, rainy and dry, and we too have two seasons, stormy and less stormy, which may be what sends so many of us to our sister archipelago. Actually, there is one spot on Kauai that can beat our 70 inches of rain a year. It's Mt. Waialeale, with an average rainfall of 426 inches (about 40 feet). It's one of the wettest spots on earth. No one lives there.

I think reflecting on our commonalities might soothe those of us *not* cashing in airline mileage to Honolulu this winter. There are plenty of similarities between our islands. Both Kodiak and Hawaii are green year-round. But because our green is that of moss and spruce trees and the color of our ocean under gray clouds, it's easy to find yourself poring over airline fares late at night in March. Or October. Or Sunday.

My sister was once so consumed by the Hawaiian Islands that she considered throwing a theme party—Hawaii in Kodiak, with luau props and blast heaters and a giant rental tent (to keep out the rain) on the beach.

"Am I crazy?" she e-mailed.

Yes. But then, most Alaskans feel a little crazy by the time daylight has dwindled to four hours a day. In the end, she didn't throw the party. Instead, she used a companion fare to book her second trip to Hawaii this year.

Humans aren't the only ones making an annual trip from here to there. Humpback whales feast on krill and small fish in Alaska waters during summer months before traveling three thousand miles to the Hawaiian Islands where they behave much like tourists, leaping and singing and breeding in the warm, clear water. The Pacific golden plover, a speckled brown shorebird with twiggy legs and a short bill, makes the same trip. The plover sounds like a beachcomber whistling for a dog. Run-stop-run, that's how plovers move on land. Plovers are born running, foraging even as their siblings are still pecking their way out. The other day I suggested to Peter that we sign up to run the Honolulu or Kauai marathon next year as a vacation excuse.

"Wouldn't that be fun?" I said.

"Or how about we just go there," he replied, "and skip the running 26.2 miles part. I'm pretty sure that would be more fun."

Along with Pacific golden plovers, Kodiak offers birders more than 240 species. Birding here might be less pleasant than in Hawaii, but more varieties of birds have gone extinct from the Hawaiian Islands than in all of North America. With that kind of survival rate, it makes you wonder. One bird on their endangered list is the Hawaiian creeper, a tiny finch found only on the Hawaiian Islands. It's about the size of the claw of our most famous endemic species, the Kodiak brown bear. One birding site warns that the Hawaiian creeper is "easily overlooked," which may be why its population has declined almost to extinction, while our hard-to-ignore, thousand-pound bears are thriving on protected refuge land that covers two-thirds of Kodiak Island.

Peter and I visited the USS *Arizona* Memorial in Hawaii last winter (the visit to Hawaii that prompted all this rumination about the relationship we Kodiak Islanders have with our Hawaiian Island brothers). Visiting Pearl Harbor made me realize how seldom we think about the Pacific War connection between Kodiak and other Pacific islands. After the bombing of Pearl Harbor, Kodiak was the site of a joint operations center, but soldiers never faced an enemy invasion here. There are bunkers along the cliffs around Kodiak where men watched for Japanese ships and submarines that never came. I used to wonder how those GIs felt about being stationed in Kodiak rather than some white-sand Bali Ha'i setting. Then I read a few of their diaries in the library archives.

"The sun was shining but still it was plenty cold out. Came in after guard hungry as the devil and all they had was salmon. I have had my full of them damn things," wrote Edmund Smith, stationed at Kodiak's Fort Greely in 1942. "A hell of a day. Was snowing and sleeting when we left. The wind was so strong that three or four times we layed on the ground to keep from blowing over. The hail came so hard it drew blood on a couple of fellows' faces...Had on water repelling clothes and the heavy Alaskan raincoat and still was wet clear through."

Reading that, you'd never know that the weather on Kodiak Island is less severe than winter weather in most of Alaska. In winter the temperature here rarely dips below zero. I try to remind myself of that—especially from November to March—when I am pining for Kauai and searching for things to appreciate about Kodiak. We owe our mild climate to the Japan Current while Hawaiians owe their economy to Japanese currency...which is much more tenuous, if you ask me.

Kodiak Island is glacier-carved with a snaking coastline. Hawaii is volcanic, eliciting all sorts of tourism dollars from people who want to see molten lava hissing into the ocean. Lava is neat, but eventually the present-day Hawaiian Islands will be worn down to nothing and all the while Kodiak Island will have been rising thanks to tectonic uplift. People here might finally be able to say that Kodiak is the biggest island in the United States, while the Hawaiians will likely be gone (just like all their birds). By then, global warming and ocean acidification will have wiped out the entire fishing industry that keeps this small town alive. Still, we will have lasted longer and won that little competition.

On Captain Cook's famous last journey, he saw Kodiak Island and the Hawaiian, or "Sandwich," Islands on the same trip. Cook named the body of water to the northeast of Kodiak "Sandwich" as well, but it was renamed Prince William Sound. Cook was honoring his financial sponsor, the Earl of Sandwich, but imagine if those names had stuck. We'd associate several famous Pacific spots with either a utensil-free lunch staple or with the sandwich's namesake, John Montague the fourth Earl of Sandwich—a drinker, gambler, and member of a group that allegedly worshipped Satan and had ritualistic sex with virgins.

Journals from men on the *Discovery* and the *Resolution* described the area around Kodiak as barren and dreary, and the air as raw and cold, even though they passed through here in the summertime, our most agreeable season. Captain Clerke noted "foul wind," "confounded fog," and "wretched weather." The Sandwich Islands garnered much more favorable descriptions in crewmen's journals than the Kodiak Archipelago did, up until Cook was stabbed to death and cannibalized on a Hawaiian beach and the sailors had to write about being given "five pounds of human flesh which they told us was Capt Cook's."

Before that, crewmen described Hawaii's enchanting climate where "we had almost every thing we could wish for, in great profusion." They wrote about the hogs and fowl, plantains, yams, and sugar cane. Though there were plenty of seals and whales around Kodiak, the main food mentioned from the area was ducks and geese, halibut and cod. They caught so much cod they complained, though not as passionately as they protested eating walrus meat in following months—this in spite of the fact that maggots were into the beef and pork, and rats and weevils were eating the bread so that "the one was little better than putrid flesh, and the other, upon breaking, would crumble into dust." Today, the primary food item our islands share in common is Spam, a salty, pink precooked meat product, also known as "the Hawaiian steak." In Kodiak, it's a fisherman's staple: fried with eggs, baked on pizza, or sliced into sandwiches.

Around 1815, while men in the Russian-American Company suffered from scurvy and starvation in the Alaska colonies, RAC employee George Scheffer was building a fort on verdant Kauai and dreaming of taking over all of the Hawaiian Islands for a new Russian colony. After alienating both King Kamehameha and RAC officials, Scheffer was finally forced to flee paradise in a leaky boat, which still seems preferable to being shipwrecked in Unalaska.

The night before we left Hawaii, my husband rolled over in bed and touched my shoulder. "Are you crying?" he asked.

"No. Yes. A little," I admitted. To get home, we flew all night and straggled through the door with car seats, sandy diaper bags, pineapples, and a tan we would relish for at least ten days. I was a bit down for a while—coconuts and sun and surfers make for an enticing way of life. So the other day I took my lunch to Fort Abercrombie. I sat on an old World War II cannon and ate my sandwich with gloves on because it was windy and cold, relishing the slices of avocado I'd paid several dollars for at the grocery store as opposed to fifty cents at a roadside stand laden with passion fruit, guava, and coconut. I watched gulls hovering over the rocks as a fishing boat sliced through three shades of blue.

I was thinking about all the things we stay here for—family, fishing, good friends, the beauty in front of me—and wondering if we'd ever be brave or foolish enough to give it all up for a gentler climate, one conducive to bare feet, or even just a place that doesn't require ice cleats and cause seasonal affective disorder. I don't like to admit it, but sometimes I want to be an Alaskan who lives outside of Alaska. Say, in Hawaii.

winter in june

I MOURN FOR THINGS I haven't lost yet. The big love of toddlers, our ten-year-old Lab, storytelling uncles and aunts who send dishtowels embroidered with each day of the week. Even our ancient fridge. Black and bulky, it takes up half the wall. But at night, when the house goes quiet, it murmurs like crickets, so that when I pass the darkened kitchen on my way to bed, I don't live on a rainy island in Alaska. I hear crickets, and I'm walking through dry grass on a hot summer night.

In winter, I grieve for lost light. This usually starts in January, when the cheer of holidays, first snows, and Christmas lights have faded. We go to work and return home in the dark. Our windows may as well be walls. The car fills with single gloves and frozen socks, a brown banana peel, and I don't notice them for weeks. Our few hours of sun are watered down and weak. Heatless.

Scrolling through digital photos, I realize how few pictures I take between November and February, unhappy with the glare of indoor flash, uninspired. Lack, by definition, is the "absence or deficiency of something needed," and it turns out I need sunlight to feel content. All winter, lacking daylight, it's as if my vision is impaired, as if I've forgotten to wear my glasses for months.

I miss light that takes up physical space, chunks of it traveling through glass onto the floor, light that spills and fills long rectangles and rests on furniture. Rays of light that transform air, the kind that Liam, when he was little, would try to catch by the handful. All winter, the light is missing. It is missed.

June in Kodiak is a month of endless light. Even after midnight, the sun softens more than sets. But one hundred years ago, late in the afternoon on June 6, 1912, daylight was snuffed out completely. There was no sound to warn Kodiak's eight hundred residents of Novarupta's eruption one hundred miles to the north, though the explosion was heard as far away as Juneau and Fairbanks. The only hint was a massive black cloud, fanning upward and outward as it traveled across Shelikof Strait. Lightning and thunder are rare here, so people were alarmed by the flashing, rumbling sky that afternoon. But they expected the cloud to pass over, and when the first soft powder began to fall, they scooped it up with teaspoons, thinking they might want to save some, unaware the town would soon be buried in ash.

By 7:00 p.m., the ash fall was so thick that it blotted out the sun. People couldn't see lanterns an arm's length away. They fought to breathe the ash-choked air. Lightning struck the wireless telegraph tower on nearby Woody Island, burning down the town's sole source of communication. Ship radios failed because of static electricity. Kodiak was cut off from the world.

"While we were at dinner the sky became black as ink," wrote W. J. Erskine, who had bought the Alaska Commercial Company holdings in Kodiak and ran a general store and fuel dock. "By nine o'clock the pumice and sand was three inches thick and the air was suffocating."

Jessie Petellin, a young woman in the village of Afognak, wrote in her account, "It began to get dark and the people became frightened and hurried to church. The old women put on their best clothes and prepared to die."

John Orloff, an Afognak resident fishing on the mainland during the eruption, wrote this letter to his wife.

My Dear Wife Tania:

First of all I will let you know of our unlucky voyage. I do not know if we will be alive and well. Every minute we are awaiting death. Of course don't be alarmed. A hill has erupted near here. So it is covering us with ashes. In some places 6 ft. and 10 ft. deep. All this began on the 6th of June. Night and day we light lamps. One cannot see daylight. In one word it is horrible, and we are awaiting death every minute. And we have no wate[r]. Here it is dark and hell. Thunder noise. I do not know whether it is night or day . . . . So kissing and blessing you both, goodbye. Forgive me. Maybe we shall see each other again. God is Merciful. Pray God For us.

Your Husband,

John Orloff

P.S. The earth is trembling every minute. It is terrible. We are praying.

The *Dora*, a mail steamer traveling from Uyak Bay to Kodiak, was just a few miles from the harbor that evening when it had to turn back to the open sea because all navigational landmarks were hidden from view. The ship's log reads, "We were in complete darkness, not even the water over the ship's side could be seen."

J. E. Thwaites, mail clerk on the *Dora*, chronicled the eruption, "As far as seeing or hearing the water, or anything pertaining to earth, we might as well have been miles above the surface of the water. Birds floundered, crying wildly, through space, and fell helpless on the deck."

Cabins struck by lightning caught fire and burned to the ground, unseen by those just a few hundred feet away. Roofs collapsed, and houses filled with landslides of ash. Hildred D. Erskine, a teacher at the territorial school in Kodiak and W. J. Erskine's sister-in-law, wrote, "No one who has not passed through such a horror-producing cataclysm can realize what it is to have the feeling that you were going to be buried alive, all the while being hemmed in by a blackness such as you had never previously known and from which there seemed to be no escape."

On June 8, after two days of darkness, people held wet rags over their mouths against the smell of sulfur and followed the summoning church bells and the whistle of the revenue cutter *Manning*, docked in front of town. Some carried lanterns; some traced their way along fences or roped themselves together. Men on board the *Manning* kept colliding as they worked to shovel ash from the deck. The ash sliced their eyes.

"The people came aboard panic stricken," wrote Nellie Erskine, W. J.'s wife. "The next day was another tough one for us. Captain Perry came and said if we don't get this ship cleaned out we will all be sick. The filth on the berth deck is frightful." Nellie sent for supplies like muslin and cornstarch from the warehouse. "The children had not been washed or their diapers changed for five days."

Eventually, the entire town evacuated. Five hundred people were packed on the deck of the *Manning;* the rest boarded the tugboat *Printer* and the coal barge the *St. James*. They anchored off Woody Island, a few miles from town, weary and crowded on board, to wait out the largest volcanic eruption of the twentieth century.

◎◎

By February, I lose all perspective. I'm bewildered by the rage that wells up as I try to buckle stiff car seat straps over Luke's snowsuit while he cries about the cold and a passing truck coats my back with slush, or when I find myself cursing frozen door handles and the snowplow that knocked off the side view mirror, or crying at random magazine articles about warmer climates. And then I recognize the symptoms of seasonal affective disorder, which arrives so consistently since we've moved back to Alaska that it's almost reassuring to name it. The feelings are as familiar as the Billie Holiday lines, "Might as well get used to you hanging around. Good morning heartache, sit down."

I take fish oil and vitamin D, sit in front of a light box, and resolve to get out and exercise, a challenge as walls of snow bury all sidewalks, trails are icy, and winter blues rob me of energy by pitch-black 5:00 p.m. I turn to books like Rick Bass's *Winter* and Edwin Way Teale's *Wandering through Winter*, hoping for insight to help me embrace the season. They seem at ease in the cold, but I can't steal their enthusiasm. In "A Winter Walk," Henry David Thoreau wrote, "Our hearts are warm and cheery, like cottages under drifts...The imprisoning drifts increase the sense of comfort which the house affords, and in the coldest days we are content to sit over the hearth and see the sky through the chimney top."

Even cozied up with a glass of dark red wine by the woodstove, I am not among the "we" comforted by "imprisoning drifts" of snow. I am only imprisoned. I want commiseration—John Updike describing winter's cold as an absence that feels more like "a vigorous, hostilely active presence," or Barry Lopez in *Arctic Dreams*, writing of the way "winter darkness shuts off the far view. The cold drives you deep into your clothing, muscles you back into your home. Even the mind retreats into itself."

For two days, those living on Woody Island hid indoors, listening to thunder and the "thumping on the windows of some little birds that had been attracted by the lamplight, trying to find refuge from the storm," George A. Learn wrote in the *Orphanage News Letter*. They had no way to communicate and were in dire need of fresh water and medical attention when they were finally picked up by the fishing boat the *Norman*. Another hundred villagers from the Alaska Peninsula were evacuated to Afognak Island. George Kosbruk was a child living near Katmai during the eruption and remembered the rescue ship arriving. "We all boarded the boat. To where? China? We had no slight idea of where they were taking us. We felt pretty safe though. Looking back, our home was disappearing where we had enjoyed our life."

Crossing Shelikof Strait, the water's surface was hidden by a seemingly solid stretch of floating pumice. "Just previous to the darkness, pumice stone began to fall, some stones fall just as big as the biggest potato you could possibly imagine," recalled Harry Kaiakokonok, a child evacuated from Kaflia village on the mainland. "Boat was like coming across dry land. All those stuff was floating on bay, about six feet deep. Dead whales and sea lions and salmons were all mixed up in those stuff floating on top of the bay."

On Kodiak, the ash from Novarupta filled shallow lakes, destroyed salmon runs for years to come, ruined water mains, and smothered the new summer growth under layers of gray. Kodiak looked lunar. In places the ash formed drifts reaching to the rooftops. Some decided to move away from Kodiak, certain that the land and town were ruined.

"Poor old Kodiak, it certainly is a wreck," Nellie Erskine wrote in a letter home. "Whether the people can live there is not at all settled. Of course it will take time and patience. It certainly is awfully discouraging, but we are not worrying. The feeling of thankfulness is too strong yet. The ashes are about two feet on the level but in places it is higher than your head. People are dazed, dirty and despondent, but I guess we can make something out of it...Baby is all well and strong and I am only tired."

The poet John Haines described being Alaskan this way: "Closeness is needed, long residence, intimacy of a sort that demands a certain daring and risk: a surrender, an abandonment, or just a sense of somehow being stuck with it."

I was born in Kotzebue to parents who took their first teaching job in Deering in the middle of winter 1972, where they melted drinking water from blocks of river ice in a fifty-five-gallon drum. Northern Alaska was where my family was made—Mom in labor on the back of a snowmachine, carrying her babies inside her parka on ice fishing trips. I spent my toddler years in a snowsuit. I admire my parents' enthusiasm and the way they make the best of each season. It's probably why I used to believe that real Alaskans earned summer by toughing out the other eight to ten months without complaining. I disliked people who were negative about Kodiak or Alaska, especially anyone who came here from somewhere else.

But now I believe you can be loyal and love something—your spouse, your job, your children—and still admit there are challenges. You can love a place, with all the allegiance of a life or childhood spent here, and appreciate the natural beauty and the friends who bring dinner when your babies are born, without loving *everything* about that place. Without loving winter.

"Before the air finally cleared," noted Robert Griggs, director of the National Geographic Society Katmai expeditions, "Kodiak had experienced two days and three nights of practically unbroken darkness." Griggs's studies of the 1912 eruption in Alaska captivated the American imagination with photos of the ashen landscape and men cooking cornbread and bacon over fumaroles in the Valley of Ten Thousand Smokes, spurring the creation of Katmai National Monument.

Most people in Kodiak returned home within a week of the eruption, digging to their doorways through knee-deep ash. They found that most of their chickens and ducks had died, but the dairy cows were spared. Some homes were ruined, like one little house near the hillside, where all that was visible through the windows was the top of the piano and the pictures hanging on the wall. Nellie Erskine described the slow return to normal life in a letter home: "Of course the place is most desolate... when you think of Kodiak, the garden spot of Alaska, it is surely enough to make you weep."

The U.S. Revenue Service kept a boat stationed in Kodiak, and ships arrived with supplies from Seattle. Little by little, rain cleaned the hillsides, though in places it turned the ash to quicksand. Rescuers worked for hours to help a man who'd been trapped, but he was blue by the time they got him out and he died soon after. Because there were no berries and salmon couldn't make it up ash-filled spawning streams, the bears were hungry and preyed on cattle and sheep.

"To everyone who visited Kodiak during the first two seasons after the eruption, the damage done to vegetation seemed irreparable," reported Robert Griggs. Yet when he returned in June 1915, he wrote, "I could not believe my eyes. It was not the same Kodiak that I had left two years before. The mountains were everywhere green with their original verdure.... Where before had been barren ash was now rich grass as high as one's head."

There is a shift from winter to the possibility of spring that has nothing to do with temperature and everything to do with the quality of light. Boats delivering loads of pollock or cod are coated in ice, but the ocean around them is finally more blue than gray. The mountains shimmer, and when snow falls on sunny days, it's lazy and weightless, like movie-set snow.

"Come in here and take a look at this, Sara!" Dad calls when I stop by. He pulls his lettuce starts from under the grow light. Dad was raised on a farm in California. Around this time of year he gets a gardening gleam in his eye. He can taste them already, the first ripe tomato, the grilled zucchini. Soon he'll be puttering around the front yard, inspecting the rhubarb and hunting for slugs with his grandsons. In the kitchen, Mom is transplanting spindly green sweet peas, their fragrance and flowers hidden within like a promise.

It feels as if Kodiak is being returned to us. We can see again—the faces of other drivers, a winter's worth of litter, our driveways and lawns and flowerbeds. Old men start running again, with awkward gaits you marvel at in admiration, and teenagers preen on sidewalks, self-conscious and delighted to be seen.

Liam and Luke play outside for hours, rediscovering mud puddles and toys lost to the snow months ago, collecting sticks and spruce cones with squirrel-like efficiency. They fight bedtime because it isn't dark yet. Last Sunday morning was so warm through the windows that Luke stripped naked, leapt off furniture for a while and then settled down next to the dog napping on a sunny section of the rug. I am irrationally happy when I wake up to a bright morning. It's as though the light brings a hopefulness I can't force in winter months. And it doesn't matter now, because I believe in summer again. The weather forecast is calling for mixed rain and snow, and we are months away from green, but I don't think about that. The feeling of thankfulness is too strong yet.

hometown ode

"SEVEN P.M. and still light! Feels like spring," Peter says after dinner. And it does feel like spring, as long as you don't compare this to spring anywhere south of here. There isn't color yet, or warmth. This spring is best through the window. Don't think about what was blooming when you were in Seattle this time last year—creamy pink magnolias and daphne sweeter than a good night's sleep. I will settle for gaining daylight. When the sun is shining, I drive squinting into it instead of pushing down the car visor and I drink my coffee wherever the square of sunshine falls in our living room. I'll drink a cup of coffee with my eyes closed if I have to, just to feel the sun on my face.

I once spent a semester in Guatemala with Amy, a friend from Texas. Whenever we walked in Antigua, I crossed to the sunny side of the street. Amy preferred the shade. A few years ago she moved to Fairbanks, Alaska, and she called me in January to say, "Remember how you always wanted to walk in the sunlight? I understand that now."

It must have been a rare, brilliant day in Kodiak when nature writer John Burroughs, friend of Walt Whitman and a member of the 1899 Harriman Expedition, set eyes on the island and wrote, "Our stay of five days in this charming place was a dream of rural beauty and repose: warm summer skies above us, green flower-strewn hills and slopes around us, our paths were indeed in green pastures and beside still waters." He went on, "So secluded, so remote, so peaceful, such a mingling of the domestic, the pastoral, the sylvan, with the wild and rugged; such emerald heights, such flowery vales, such blue arms and recesses of the sea, and such a vast green solitude stretching away to the west and the north and to the south! Bewitching Kodiak, the spell of thy summer freshness and placidity is still upon me."

Caroline Erskine, in a memoir about growing up here in the late 1800s, wrote of holding the canvas for Jan Van Empel, a visiting Dutch painter, while he painted outdoors. "I remember that intoxicating west wind as a dramatic and exhilarating experience for it seemed to blow everything before it, cleansing the air and giving you a feeling that, with the will to do so, you could soar off and tumble with the clouds."

There are days I struggle for even a sliver of such enthusiasm. "Remind me again why we moved back here?" I'll ask Peter as we add up our fuel and grocery bills or scroll through photos his sister, Carrie, e-mails from Florida. "Wait, go back one photo. Is that a coconut tree *in their backyard*?"

Peter and I grew up on Kodiak but left for colleges on opposite sides of the country. Most Kodiak kids leave after high school, and many settle outside of Alaska, but quite a few eventually move back to raise their families here. For a few years, Peter and I spent summers fishing in Uyak and winters traveling or living in the Southwest or Seattle. That worked pretty well when it was just the two of us, but when Liam was a year old, we moved to Kodiak year-round. It meant giving up nightly options of live music and take-out, but we also traded hour-long commutes for grandparents five minutes away.

We spent that first winter renovating our first house, and when we finally moved in, the best part of unpacking was opening the boxes of books I'd lugged between states for ten years. As I filled the bookshelves, I stopped and sat down with Pablo Neruda's poetry. Each time I read his odes—to the artichoke, to laziness, his socks, a yellow bird, salt, lemons, his suit, to ironing, to the onion—I am convinced that such exuberance is easier to come by in hot climates. Yet as I thought about what pieces of everyday beauty I might find for an ode to Kodiak, I noticed that I paid more attention to things, like the island scent of wet moss and low tide and rained-on spruce trees. I don't need to write as effusively as Neruda or Burroughs, I'd just rather not spend years blaming my husband every time it snows in April.

My ode to Kodiak would be color pocketed like pieces of beach glass—the blue domes of the Russian Orthodox Church, pink buoys in crab pots stacked around town, a bouquet of imported daffodils opening a sunny yellow on my kitchen table, the unexpected color of glossy vegetables in three seed catalogs that arrived on the same rainy day last week. We woke recently to the year's brightest full moon over the lavender peaks of Three Sisters; by afternoon the mountains blazed white against the pewter sky. At night there is the candle-warm light on the masts of fishing boats. Looking down from the bridge on an evening walk, the light spills from boat decks and casts a broken path over the water.

An ode to woods that are hushed and lush green even as storms blow a melancholy song through the treetops. These are storybook forests, thick with moss and lichens and spruce that make it easy to imagine bears behind every other tree, or fairies and trolls.

An ode to birds like the flame-breasted varied thrushes at the feeder and the black-and-white harlequins gliding by Fuller's boatyard. All month across the channel, a convocation of eagles has been solemnly overseeing cod production at the canneries. They're plentiful as pigeons, but we have pigeons here too, inexplicably at home in downtown Kodiak. The startling waves of gray birds downtown reminds me momentarily of piazzas in Italy each time I glimpse their flurry of wings, before they settle back down onto our low, square office buildings. And yesterday when my son pressed the audio button for the golden crown sparrow at the wildlife refuge center, summer in Kodiak was tangible, if only for the length of its song.

An ode then, even to the rain, for easing the strain on deer and our furnaces. Rain that washes away the slush. Rain that assures we'll never be overrun with tourists because you have to really love it here to see past the stormy days. To rain that ended just long enough for me to carry my last box of books up the slippery steps, grateful for good knees and words that sustain us through cold winter days and for clear skies that renew and rejuvenate, like the summer season we are waiting for.

sea chains broken

EVERY WEDNESDAY at 2:00 p.m., a tsunami siren wakes napping babies and sets dogs howling, reminding us that Kodiak lies on the Pacific Ring of Fire, one of the most active seismic regions in the world. I've read that more than 70 percent of the world's tsunamis occur in the Pacific Ocean and that these waves may hit coasts as soon as fifteen minutes after an earthquake or as long as twenty-four hours later. Tsunamis can hit without warning, like the deadly waves that have reached Hawaii from earthquakes in Chile and the Aleutian Chain and the 2004 Indian Ocean tsunami that killed more than two hundred thousand. When I was growing up on Kodiak, earthquakes and evacuations were fairly common, but I didn't really understand how tsunamis worked. I pictured a single curling wave, like a Hokusai print, that would sweep the village clean, leaving a smooth stretch of land.

Kodiak's 1964 tsunami arrived as a series of waves that rearranged the town, washing boats from the harbor into neighborhoods and dragging houses and buildings into the ocean. Before the sun set the night of March 27 and hid all but the tremendous noise, people watched as the first waves coursed in and out of the channel. "Every once in awhile someone in the crowd on the shore would cry out as he recognized a certain store, or house, or boat being swept by on the relentless waves," recalled Pastor Lautaret.

Mary Cichoski's dad was on his fishing boat during the earthquake, far enough offshore that he didn't feel the ocean rise or know of the disaster until he returned to Kodiak and found his house floating in the channel. "He didn't know if his family had gotten out or not," Mary said, "so the first thing he did was tie up to the house and go inside and check it out. He tried to tow the house with his boat, but it didn't work."

The tsunami followed a 9.2 earthquake, the second largest in recorded history. Just over one hundred people died that night in Alaska, almost all of them killed by the resulting waves. Alaska's sparse population is often mentioned as preventing a higher death toll, but in villages like Chenega Bay, where the tsunami took one-third of the village, almost everyone lost a relative. Eighteen people died in Kodiak—a village chief, a little brother on a camping trip, a wife pulled from her husband's arms.

Boats ran aground as fishermen tried—too late—to flee before the ocean drained out of the harbor. Then the water returned, ramming boats into floats, sinking some and spinning others into the channel. Many fishermen who'd rushed to their boats just after the earthquake expected the waves to weaken; instead, ensuing waves peaked in height and strength around 11:00 p.m., arriving hourly until four in the morning.

John Reft, a teenager in 1964, ran to the dock with his cousin just after the earthquake and tried to convince his dad to head for higher ground. His dad decided to ride out the tsunami on the boat, heading into the channel with six men on board. They made it over the first few waves before his voice came over the CB radio a final time: "Here comes the third one. It's a big one, don't look like we'll make it through this one." Their bodies were never found. The tsunami claimed victims as far away as Oregon and California.

We often borrow the vocabulary of natural disasters for overwhelming events—things shake our foundation, flood over us. Kodiak accounts of the earthquake and tsunami are full of similes, as people try to describe an experience so beyond control it seemed that it could not have been happening—sound roaring through the ground, crawling for the door because it was impossible to stand.

"The trees were like fishing poles when you jiggle them real fast."

"The ice broke up in Dark Lake and was swishing around like in a martini glass."

Mooring lines snapping "like a thousand guns going off."

Maybe such comparisons are a way of fitting an experience into the shelter of language. What all the Kodiak accounts share in common is their ordinary beginning—the stories always start before the earth began shaking, before the waves. They begin in an innocence impossible to return to except in the retelling:

"We were coloring Easter eggs at the time."

"I had been working down at the cannery."

"I was just about to go outside and feed the chickens."

"We had just gotten home from Mass," Thelma Johnson remembered. "We looked out and could see the wires slapping together and sparks flying. The children had a little playhouse outdoors and a little girl was out there and she was hammering a nail in the wall hanging a picture in the playhouse and all of a sudden she came crawling out and saying, 'I didn't do it, I didn't do it.'"

If we're lucky, we spend so much of our life in ordinary days that we don't even think to note what we were doing or how we passed the time. And then something catastrophic happens, and in stories told later, the routine is captured too, and it is somehow more precious, set against chaos. After an event shakes us from dailyness, the ordinary is what we want most to return to.

Maybe that's why people here rebuilt in the same places, or maybe it's indicative of the reckless optimism of this fishing town. In a coincidence that became a town joke, the night before the earthquake, city officials attended a planning and zoning meeting to discuss an urban renewal project for downtown Kodiak. The next day, said Judge Roy Madsen, "the tidal wave came in and accomplished a lot of the basic work." Amid the rubble, people found yards of fabric from the dry goods store, hundreds of whiskey bottles from downtown bars, and cans of food without labels they were warned not to eat. Charles Madsen, who was ten years old, remembers digging in the mud for the silver balls of pinball machines near the remains of the arcade and pool hall.

Once the wreckage was cleared away and curfews to prevent looting were lifted, after electricity and heat were restored, drinking water was deemed safe, and schools and businesses reopened, Kodiak was reborn with wide, straight roads in place of winding lanes. A modern town, rather than a pastoral fishing village.

@@

When Peter and I went back to our favorite coastal town in Thailand a year after the 2004 tsunami, we walked for miles along the water, where the only remaining things were empty blue-tiled swimming pools, like fallen squares of sky. We passed a memorial to a toddler with a photo of a chubby, blue-eyed boy, a candle, a plastic dinosaur. At the time, I was newly married. I felt sad for the family, but I couldn't imagine the grief of going back or of going forward. And now that I have little blue-eyed boys of my own, how easily I see it. How brief is the time we feel invulnerable to loss.

Watching the unfolding of earthquakes, floods, and accidents from our homes half a country or world away, we are reminded of the random nature of such violence. When I follow reports and images of rescue workers digging through the wreckage, I am always hoping for small miracles—the baby found floating on a mattress, unhurt, in Port Alberni after the 1964 tsunami hit Vancouver Island. I'm fascinated by the destructive power of nature, but I also want a glimpse of bravery or survival or simple human kindness.

"During the quake and wave I came into the house and got a pair of Jack's socks and gave them to a man. He sat down in the yard and put them on. Then I gave someone a coat. I didn't even know who they were," wrote Betty Metzger in a fifteen-page letter just after the disaster.

After the tsunami, City Hall printed dispatches to keep the community informed because Kodiak's newspaper building had been destroyed. Those first weeks the daily headings read EVACUATION, CURFEW, TYPHOID IMMUNIZATIONS, CASUALTIES, STILL MISSING, but there were also sections for GOOD NEWS and ODDITY: "The home of Clayton Copsey at the Small Boat Harbor was swept to a point back of the old school. An Easter lily rode on the smooth top table and was blooming unconcernedly when Bill Stone found it on

Monday. It, and some Easter bread, seemed to have never moved an inch. Bill feels this is a real good omen."

We salvage through stories. A year has passed since the last big tsunami destroyed cities in Japan. We've followed the news of debris traveling over the Pacific Ocean to the coasts of Alaska and California. We've been told to expect millions of tons of wreckage—boats and parts of houses, shoes with feet still inside. Dozens of Japanese oyster farm buoys that were dislodged in the tsunami have already washed up on Kodiak. All over the news today is the story of a soccer ball found on a beach in Alaska. The ball was lost in the tsunami and is being returned to the sixteen-year-old boy in Japan whose name is still legible on its side. The soccer ball is not the treasure; the story is.

We were in Hawaii during that same tsunami last spring. For several hours, our family watched footage from Japan in disbelief. It was a strange experience to see the destruction and follow the progress of approaching waves traveling across the Pacific. After evacuating, we spent a night huddled on the floor of the rental van in the post office parking lot.

I've always liked thinking about the connections between Pacific islands—beachcombing for Japanese fishing floats, reading about sailors adrift in lifeboats. Here was an immediate correlation—as I carried my sleeping one-year-old to the car, grateful to be safe and with my family, I ached for mothers in Japan shushing their children in shelters, holding babies in line for radiation screenings, searching for sons and daughters in the wreckage. An unsought connection and the knowledge hidden within the shelter of our stories—that in the face of waves strong enough to reach across oceans, we are all so fragile.

sea chains broken

fifteen times over the bridge

I

WE LIVE UP THE HILL from the only large bridge on the island of Kodiak. It's no architectural masterpiece, just a steel bridge built twenty-five years ago to connect the city to the St. Herman boat harbor on Near Island. As kids, we rode bikes across to feed carrots and old lettuce to a herd of half-wild ponies.

It's an easy ten minutes over and back to get our dog out to do his business. He's a considerate dog and always waits for the alders and gravel on the other side. I wish that were true of all the dogs on the pedestrian walkway. The bridge was under construction when firefighters toured local elementary schools with their new Dalmation puppy. Kids suggested names, and the winning name, Hoser, made Travis Diemer the envy of his second-grade class.

Hoser was the first bridge death. His was an enthusiastic, rather than desperate, jump. For a few years, the bridge was called Hoser's Bridge before it was renamed for a local politician. This is how it goes, walking over the bridge and following thoughts as skittish as the pigeons lined up on a ledge beneath me. This walk is my favorite thinking time. Maybe my only thinking time some days. Between the toddler and the baby, I rarely make it out until the evening, when I realize I have let the whole day slip by and if I don't run out the door I will not have had three minutes alone, in fresh air.

II

I should have brought a pen and paper for the thoughts rattling around in my head. The wind through the chain-link fence makes the storm sound worse than it is. Like an early morning after a long night, the baby a hungry human metronome and Liam up with a nightmare at 3:00 a.m. After such nights, my feelings catch on a sharp word and Peter and I haggle over who got to shower, who finished their whole cup of coffee.

Someone spray-painted on the bridge years ago: *don't leave me babe*. It sounds like an old song. Like our town, back when fishing was making everyone rich. Before I was married, I loved pet names like "babe." Hearing those names from a boyfriend felt like belonging. I've known my husband since we were kids. Maybe we always belonged in some familiar way, and so we didn't need such names. What in that graffiti makes me wistful? The carelessness of leaving? Belonging, before I understood what the word requires?

The channel is teal, a color I loved when I was younger. And purple. Together. I loved them until I couldn't stand them. Every time I describe the channel that way in writing my husband suggests that I cut the word *teal*. I always do. But not today. Today that water is so teal it actually looks inviting, delicious, like it might taste like gazpacho. Teal soup.

III

We are standing on Near Island under a seashell of sky, a conch pink sunset at our backs. Liam is crushing frozen puddles. I watch the round bubbles under the ice, the arc of these frozen lines broken into shards and jagged shapes beneath his boots, from circles to triangles. There must be significance in that—splintering round into angles, but no. There is purpose enough in this innocent breaking, a small boy intent on claiming every last puddle.

IV

Soft air, soft fog, light melting into the dark, wet evening. Winter is so often harsh and stinging. "I like it best when it mists," a local Kodiak girl told Isobel Hutchinson, a visiting Scottish botanist, as they hiked up Pillar Mountain in 1936. "You feel as if you belonged to nothing then." The fog has hushed everything—boats and cars and the commerce going on along the water under the bridge even at this late hour. Fog hides the Russian Orthodox Seminary below. I always appreciate the little wooden church with its gold stars painted on royal blue domes. Almost anything pretty in this town is nature-made.

Sometimes I wonder what keeps people here. If I kept walking down the road, I would come to a gaping gravel pit that makes Near Island look like a green cake with an enormous slice hacked out. Newly cleared lots are just starting to sell on the island, one more option for the businesses moving out of downtown. What's left downtown is a bingo hall, a dozen bars, and a few empty spaces for rent at prices too high for anyone to stay for long. We seem almost proud to be antitourism here, and after driving through the boarded-up Western set that is Skagway in the winter, I don't wish for tourist-season-only growth. It's possible that an empty downtown is truer to who we are—a row of canneries, a boat harbor, dark bars.

The fog tonight feels like kindness. A line from a T. S. Eliot poem runs through my head: "By this grace dissolved in place." I walk home soothed, knowing that once the boys are asleep there will be a few quiet hours with my husband, even if it means staying up until midnight and missed sleep we'll regret in the morning.

V

I was tricked by the sunlight pouring onto our kitchen floor. That square of blue sky was only in our windows. Now I see that the rest of the sky is a cold metallic white. It's bitter cold; it was foolish not to wear a hat. The men on the docks and fishing boats beneath the bridge are working with raw, stiff fingers.

The seagulls sound brittle. I recognize home in that sound. A sound can be a feeling too. Today the gulls are the sound of being six years old in an open skiff, eyes watering in the wind, pressed close to Mom or Dad. Their cries are a handful of round stones, a different weight for every call. The sound of gulls is the brackish smell of two-cycle exhaust from an old Evinrude.

VI

The sky is smudged graphite. Below the bridge, boat lights stretch over the water like tinsel. I am trying to run but keep slipping on ice under the slush. I give up running, picturing a spider in a bowl. Even spiders have better sense than to venture out in this weather. A tantrum day. My shirt is wet with milk. My shoes are submerged. I'm walking away from my house and already steeling myself to walk back in, to meet the two sets of needs, hungry baby, crabby toddler. Slush is exactly how I'm feeling.

VII

The sun is glaring off the mountains. I'm missing my mom, who is only away for a few weeks. I think of Liam, and how close he is to her and to all of his grandparents. Sometimes I worry that when they're gone he'll know loss in a way I didn't. Gone. I can't even say dead. I don't know what's more odd, this anticipatory mourning, or the fact that we all get through so much of the day without thinking about death and illness and all the terrible things that might happen to our families.

Sometimes the alders at the end of the bridge make me nervous that something might be hiding in there. Not a bear, more like a deranged drifter just back from the Bering Sea. Then I think of Timothy Treadwell and his girlfriend getting eaten by bears. I picture her trying to help, swinging that frying pan, and then getting eaten too, and I feel terrible for that girl. Then I wonder what the hell I'm doing, imagining that, when these are my ten minutes of peace.

I just read *Lift* by Kelly Corrigan. She writes to her daughters, "That means you won't ever know me as I am right now—the mother I am tonight and tomorrow, the mother I've been for the last eight years, every bath and book and birthday party, gone. It won't hit you that you're missing this chapter of our story until you see me push your child on a swing or untangle his jump rope or wave a bee away from his head and think, Is this what she was like with me?"

It's true; I've had that second chance to understand how much love my mom gave us during all those years I don't remember. I'm so grateful for that. Other than that, I think forgetfulness might be a blessing. I am afraid that the many things my mom notices and appreciates—spring and songbirds and flowers blooming—will all remind me of her someday, probably every day, and I'm lonesome already.

VIII

Not sunny and not stormy. Too many days of this make me blue, although blue is the wrong word. The absence of blue is the trouble. Eagles squat on every other light post along the bridge. I don't like eagles, ever since a day or two after my first son was born, when I took a slow, sore walk down the alley behind our house. A mother mallard waddled along, stopping at puddles with her two little downy babies while I stood watching, holding my own small baby to my chest. My dad reported a day later that the mother duck now had only one duckling. The following day he told me he'd watched an eagle swoop down and snatch away her remaining baby. I'm sure my hysterical crying was in large part hormonal—those first days are fragile days—but I lost all love for eagles then. I'm not sure parents ever stop worrying that some terrible thing might swoop down and hurt their children.

IX

I feel as though I control all sound tonight. There is the grate of my hurried footsteps over frozen snow and when I stop, nothing. Tonight the snow is more shadow than white. Evening-stained snow. I breathe in sips. The air stings and even my tongue is numb. During college I worked as a teacher's aide in Fairbanks, where inside recess was reserved for days colder than twenty below. I would use a numb tongue as a measure of when to bring the kids in from the playground—when it was hard to talk because I couldn't feel my tongue, it was time to go inside.

It's almost 8:00 p.m. and still light, the sky a hopeful teacup blue. I should have worn gloves. The wind hurts. My dad, who wears long johns year-round, used to scold me for not dressing for the weather. I gave up sacrificing warmth for vanity years ago, but tonight I literally had to run out the door or I knew there would be no walk, no ten minutes of calm.

The water looks painfully cold. This night reminds me why I didn't stay in Fairbanks. I hate the clenching power of cold, the temperatures that cement the world into tight stillness. On this side of the bridge a fence is meant to discourage jumpers. Because it's only on one side, the few people who *have* jumped simply crossed and leapt from the other side. They were pulled from the water, alive. They say bridge suicide is usually an impulsive act and that survivors of such jumps report regretting the decision as they fell. Of all the deterrents, like stepping off into nothing, the pain of impact, the descent, it's the shock of sinking down through that cold water that strikes me as the most repellent.

X

"Just a taste," said my mother-in-law, when our two-year-old asked for coffee after dinner. Now, at 9:00 p.m., Liam is running laps. I put Luke in the Bjorn and we walk over the bridge with our good old dog and the wild toddler in striped pajamas under a winter coat, and how can you be impatient with a kid in striped pajamas chasing an old brown Labrador? Nothing is green, it is not warm, but the light alone is enough to make us hopeful. The fog is rolling in, the sky spitting wet snow, but this is contentment—Luke blowing noises against my chest, Liam playing king of the mountain of mud and gravel before he slides down on his bottom. Later, when I put his pajamas in the washing machine, he cries. Before that, he cried about holding a hand on the sidewalk, then about being carried, then about bedtime, and I was amazed all over again at how much work this is.

XI

Peter is gone herring fishing this month. Liam spent last night in our bed throwing up into a bucket. I am not as good as I'd like to be at doing this alone. When the morning starts to make me short-tempered, I strap Luke into a pack, tuck Liam into the stroller, and hook a suitcase strap onto the dog since the leash is nowhere to be found. We stop for a long time on the middle of the bridge, watching boats pass underneath and the wind turbines spinning on Pillar Mountain. Long enough to feel peaceful again.

XII

Muddy puddles, brown hillside, bright sky. I'm running over the bridge with my eyes half closed against the sun, squinting up at eagles close enough to swat at. I am not thinking. It makes me feel young to run with music too loud and no thoughts in my head.

That's not true. I just thought about that runner in the news, the one killed in South Carolina. You're running along on a beach, pounding out happy footsteps to the beat of your iPod, and then a single-engine plane, silent without its propeller, glides in for an emergency landing right on top of you. Dead. I really want to stay alive. So I turn my music down a little and as I do, I tug my sweatshirt down in the back. These days, running again after having two children and about four years without so much as a jog, I prefer that my butt be covered. I feel a bit like those teenagers tangled up in tee-shirts worn over their swimsuits in the pool. But I am happy anyway, running in sunshine.

XIII

This afternoon I watch kayakers and the Vs of boats coming and going and the snow is nothing, just some white in the distance under all this blue sky. And though the sun is not blazing, the sunlight is brilliant, and I just know that every other person in this small northern town is feeling as giddy as I am. When I get home I will wash the windows and then the cupboards, and the snow boots we needed yesterday will look silly in a pool of sunshine. It's as though we've been stumbling blindly for months, living in the mess of winter. I forget that spring is a teasing, mercurial girl, and I am in love, and she will break my heart tomorrow with a gale or a snowstorm. Today the water is thick as green paint beneath the bridge. Fish guts from the canneries are swirling like trails of cream on coffee. Days like today it's as though we've been half alive all winter. Days like today we plan gardens and spring clean and leave work a little early and smile at neighbors and it is spring, it has to be—the whole summer has to be just as sunny and beautiful as this day is.

XIV

The roof of the last building before the channel is marked with an H. I know it's a helicopter pad but I always think of other H words as I pass over it. Halibut, happy, hello. An eagle just flew so close I could hear his feathers. During cod season, eagles are thick as bats around the bridge. I see my younger sister driving on the road below me. I wave but she doesn't look up. My sister is thinking about moving. When she asked for advice, all I could offer was that it might be easier to start over now, before she owns a house or just so much stuff that she can't imagine packing everything up. And change is usually good. But so is being content. Basically, I was no help at all. I'm not sure about settling down here either. I know that as the boys get older and start school, it will only get harder to leave. As I walked back across the bridge today after ten minutes of mountains and wind, it seemed that home was what the H stood for.

XV

Before gusts of wind turn us back halfway across the bridge, Liam chases his shadow down the walkway. Shadows are kind of a novelty here. I lift him to stand, his fingers laced through the fence, to show him the sea lion heaving itself onto a fishing boat. He asks me to set him on the cement divide between walking path and road. I hold one hand as we walk and keep the other at his back to catch him if I need to. We make slow progress, but still, he is holding my hand. All the things that drive me crazy about this age—the dawdling, the arguments about what he can do by himself and what he cries for us to do for him—are so fleeting. "I don't need you," he said to me this morning as we were making hot chocolate. He wanted to pour the milk himself. He spilled and I cleaned it up, because this is my job, to want him to do things himself, to become an independent little person. But to hear "I don't need you" was a hint of how quickly it's true, and remembering that makes me more patient as we cross the bridge hand in hand.

red caviar

AT OUR SETNET SITE, we fish nets that extend one hundred fathoms (about six hundred feet) from the shore into the path of migrating salmon. From net to net, we shake or pull salmon, one by one, until boat, boots, and faces are caked with jellyfish, fish slime, and blood. When salmon fishing is your livelihood, you don't think about the gurgling sound as you wrench a salmon from the net by its gill plates. You think about pennies per pound. The faster you pick the nets, the sooner you're done, and the more you catch, the better.

After a morning pick, our skiff cuts a straight path across the bay to the Larsen Bay cannery where our salmon are processed. The cannery comes into view like an old retouched photograph, red metal roofs crisp against gray buildings and the low gray sky. Older walls are the mottled hues of a spawned-out salmon. When we tie up at the dock, the air smells of hot creosote and brine. My husband shouts over the rumble of cannery generators that he'll find me after he drops off the mail.

I'm looking for Jade de la Paz, the supervisor of salmon roe production for Icicle Seafoods. She'd agreed to show me the egg house, a part of the cannery I was curious about after hearing fishermen describe it as a mysterious place where Japanese men in blue coveralls performed secretive work. Some of the mystery has to do with the elusive value of roe, but it's also true that fishermen tend to think in thousands of pounds of whole fish and not in handfuls of delicate, pearl-sized eggs.

The egg house is prettier than I expected—although *pretty* is not typically a cannery adjective—with its clean aqua floors and tangerine ribbons of eggs in sky-blue baskets. Here they make *ikura,* or red caviar, from the pea-sized eggs of chum and pink salmon. It's the most valuable roe product and is sold mainly to Japan. I've tried *ikura* at sushi restaurants, but the novelty of chopsticks and wasabi overshadowed it. A true *ikura* connoisseur savors the honey-like flavor and the mouth-popping feel of each egg. The smaller eggs of sockeye and coho are also processed here for cheaper products like heavily salted Japanese *sujiko,* or roe, shipped frozen in the skein.

"I feel like caviar is the forgotten child. Nobody understands the egg house," says de la Paz. "In the fish house everything is really big. With the fish, you cut them, you clean them, you put them in a box, and you're done. In the egg house everything is details, details. You really feel like in the fish house it's large-scale things. In the egg house, here's one tiny piece of caviar and it's very, very important."

Grading is a central part of producing salmon caviar. The eggs must be nearly flawless to be considered top quality, and Japanese buyers have strict standards for the *ikura* they import. Japanese buyers rarely trust Alaska processors to make salmon caviar unless Japanese technicians have supervised and graded the eggs. Like an oenologist attuned to the nuances of wine grapes, a roe technician has mastered the sensory evaluation of salmon eggs.

Salmon caviar gets two grades. Ovaries are evaluated by stages of maturity from I to VI. The most valuable eggs come from stage IV ovaries, which fill the belly cavity with single eggs that are easily detachable. Eggs from a mature salmon are brighter, bigger, and stronger than immature eggs. But if a female salmon is *too* old, her eggs may be too runny to process. When we catch a stage-VI salmon in September, the eggs sometimes squirt out when we pull her through the net. The second grade is based on the attributes of eggs after they are removed from the skein. Japanese technicians judge individual egg quality by the color, texture, size, flavor, and membrane thickness.

Salmon caviar is a simple food. It's a raw fish egg. Yet the trip from egg house to packinghouse takes three days and a staff of roe technicians, plus twenty to forty regular cannery employees. After roe is graded, it is weighed and rinsed in chlorine. Then eggs are agitated in brine before employees open and spread the salmon ovaries flat onto a conveyor belt. Like peeling open a pomegranate, this exposes the eggs once held inside a translucent membrane. They're placed skein side up for the trip through the hopper, a machine that pushes the eggs down through a sloping screen and deposits them as a flat orange sheet of individual eggs. Then workers use tweezers to pick out bits of eggshells, stringy tissue, and flecks of blood. After a second agitation, the caviar is transferred to the draining room.

When the blast of the state's oldest operating steam whistle signals "mug up," I follow de la Paz to the carts of coffee and baked goods. Workers shed their uniforms of stiff green raingear and stand around in black cannery-issued boots, eating cookies, smoking cigarettes, and speaking in Polish, Russian, Spanish, Filipino, and English. In recent years, workers from around the world have replaced the cannery staff of American college students on summer vacation.

Within that community, the Japanese roe technicians tend to keep to themselves. You don't see them playing volleyball on the sandy outdoor court or loitering around the cannery store and docks. They live communally in a small house, rather than in the dorms where other cannery employees are housed. I try several times to ask the roe technicians about their work. They seem surprised that I consider their job unusual. Each time I knock on their door and ask for an interview, I'm turned away with a polite no.

Salmon caviar cures for eight to twelve hours in the draining room before being transferred to the packing room. Walking to the packing room, I side-step a forklift and then a golf cart rattling over the boardwalk planks. They honk at every corner and doorway, weaving around aluminum skiffs dry-docked for repairs, workers on bicycles, and towers of pallets.

The packing room is full of girls. Women are often given the first shot at these positions because their hands are smaller and better able to get at the eggs, according to an online job site that describes the packing room as "less hectic than working on your average slime line." However, it warns, "Employees … should be prepared to stand at a table packing eggs into boxes for many long hours." I watch the women, their hairnets tilted down as they spread caviar into plastic containers, wondering what thoughts would sustain me if I spent the same monotonous days here. By the end of summer, because of the buckets of iodine and chlorine, you can spot a packing room girl by her bleached boots.

I didn't expect to find an *ikura* aficionado the same day I visited the egg house, especially in the village of Larsen Bay. I'd pictured these packages traveling to sushi restaurants or Japanese kitchens. But Joe Lindholm, skipper of the tender vessel *Tana C.*, which picks up salmon from seiners and setnetters and delivers it to the cannery all summer, passed us on the dock and offered to share the salmon caviar he had on the boat.

"It's an acquired taste, like scotch," says Lindholm. "It's fishy and there's a neat little pop in your mouth. It's got a different texture. I certainly wouldn't want to sit down and have it like French toast. Just a dozen little eggs on a cracker, that's just right."

I wonder if this Japanese staple could ever be an American dinner choice as ordinary as meatloaf. I try to imagine bringing raw salmon eggs to a Super Bowl party or packing them in my son's lunchbox. It seems more likely that I'll continue having *ikura* at sushi restaurants. I'll picture the Larsen Bay cannery and crews in a working meditation above the elemental form of salmon eggs taken from salmon returning to Alaska to spawn.

the simple life

WHEN PETER AND I built our cabin on Amook Island, friends expressed their envy. No roads or cars, no communication, just water and mountains and wildlife. Also, lots of dead generators and wet logs smoldering in our peckish woodstove. It's a popular idea, that giving things up is the best way to clear away the mental clutter we blame on computers, televisions, and appliances. I'm not convinced. Amazon.com offers eighteen thousand books on simple living—*Simple Living for the Worn Out Woman* and *Voluntary Simplicity* and *The Joy of Simple Living: 1,500 Simple Ways to Make Your Life Easy and Content*. I don't need such books, thanks to the involuntary simplicity imposed each year when we move to the fishsite for the salmon season.

After a lifetime of summers spent here, Peter associates the season with stormy weather, wet raingear, and eating dinner at midnight. He has never chased swallowtails with a butterfly net, tie-dyed at summer camp, played Little League baseball, or manned a lemonade stand. Until just a few years ago, he'd never mowed a lawn. He does not associate the word *lazy* with the words *summer day*. In other words, he doesn't know how summer is supposed to be. The last summer he remembers having "off" was in 1989, when he was twelve years old and the Exxon *Valdez* oil spill canceled the salmon season. Pete spent most of that June, July, and August walking the beaches of Uyak and Amook Island, picking up dead birds and otters and buckets of weathered drifting oil.

Peter's mom and dad started fishing here in 1972 with two business partners. One partner drowned while taking his skiff around the island. Henry, the other partner, spent most of his time smoking, painting things green, and watching the strawberries grow until the Danelskis bought him out in 1987. Jan, my mother-in-law, will shoot a deer that's eating out of her garden, hang it in the shed, and skin it herself, and then for a week or two she'll select the evening's meat, cutting away maggots if need be. By now, she has cooked and served salmon approximately one million times. After forty seasons here, the Danelskis aren't fazed by a summer grocery list with items like three hundred pounds of flour, or high tides that carry off the outhouse, or river otters moving in under the cabin.

We live across the bay from Peter's parents, a two-mile skiff ride that Peter likes to call his "commute." The twenty-two-foot aluminum skiff is our only means of transportation. Because of tides and rocks, it has to be pulled in and out on a running line each time we arrive and each time we leave. At the start of the summer, we think of pulling the running line as a great biceps workout. By the fall, all we can think of is how good it will be to pull a car into a parking spot. Even in good weather, skiff rides are wet, slick, bumpy, and windy. We are yet to cross the bay without one of the boys losing a tiny Xtratuf rain boot to the slurry in the bottom of the boat. Our favorite feature of child lifejackets are the handles that allow you to lift and pass dangling kids across a skiff full of salmon blood and pulverized jellyfish or to haul forty pounds of boy up the forty-two steps to the cabin.

"You live like pioneers," a relative said after visiting our fishsite. Pioneers with solar panels and a Toyo stove, but I know what she meant. Yet if we've already violated the code of the pioneer with a Netflix account, why choose to live without a dryer or microwave or telephone? Why go backward in time when all these inventions exist to make our lives easier?

This simple life could also be called the time-consuming life. You might have fewer options of things to do, but everything takes more time. I believe the tasks required to live this way used to be known as "chores." Out here, if you're hungry for something in particular, the only way to satisfy your craving is to make it yourself from scratch. I've learned from experience that with bagels and soft pretzels, you're better off going without. Cookbooks published within the past three decades aren't practical at the fishsite, as they assume you have access to fresh ingredients. A 1950s Betty Crocker is a better choice.

Some mornings Liam likes to help make breakfast. I think it's important to cook with your kids, but it *is* messy. I keep patient even as his one-handed egg-cracking technique sends yolk down the cabinet doors and shells into the mixing bowl. I feel my voice rising as he reaches into the canister for another lump of sugar to crumble onto the floor. I wipe his hands. Give him the second egg.

"Once it cracks you don't have to keep crushing the shell," I say. I would like to crack my own head and lie down for a while . . . mmmm, peace and quiet.

One confession. We do have a washing machine that runs off our generator. Thanks to a series of generator malfunctions, the washer smells like an electrical fire and shudders through its cycles half-heartedly. Toss in a folded item and thirty minutes later you'll remove a damp, folded item. But I don't have to wash our clothing in the creek that runs by our cabin, which would be truer to a simple life. Recently, a Burmese refugee told me she actually misses washing clothing in the river. I bet it was warm there. I bet the water wasn't numbing. Our creek water, even in the washing machine, is so cold it doesn't dissolve laundry soap. Unfortunately, the creek is not too cold for worms to live in. We don't have a dryer. We have a clothesline, and I think if we lived farther from the Arctic Circle I might actually enjoy hanging clothes out to dry. But heavy rainfall, fog, and mist aren't conducive to drying wet things. A windy day helps, except that our wind is frequently strong enough to whip clothing into tight beads on the line like those shellacked paper necklaces from Africa.

Another confession. We don't have an outhouse. We splurged on a composting toilet that I have never emptied. That's because I watched Peter remove what the manufacturer promised would be a tray full of clean, fluffy dirt. It wasn't dirt. We will never take their advice to sprinkle the contents of the composter over our garden. Gardening is one part of this life that seems worth the work, and I don't want to ruin it by pouring shit all over it. Then again, our "potty-trained" toddler's dubious aim has me reconsidering the merits of an outhouse. There is a mother in this bay with five sons. She refuses indoor plumbing, and I think I know why.

With the garden, I don't mind the time it takes to see results. Even when we eat nothing but root vegetables in September because that's when everything is finally ready. This is not the case with baking bread. Peter's mom cooks for the crew, and she bakes bread nearly every day. In the time it takes to wash your hands, she will have mixed and shaped several perfect loaves. Pete's twin sister, Jackie, inherited this knack. Their bread looks stolen from a picnic in France: it's right out of a Henri Cartier-Bresson photo. My loaves tend to turn out more gourd-like. Baking bread occurs to me after I've pulled out the peanut butter and jelly for an impossible sandwich because we are out of bread. Every time I measure out yeast, I realize I should have started hours before. I read the recipe and calculate—this dough will be ready to bake at approximately . . . 10:00 p.m. I grumble until I start kneading. Olive oil shines on my hands and the dough is a pleasure to hold. Liam helps snip rosemary from the plant on the windowsill and then shapes his own tiny loaf. Bread baking is a calm, welcoming scent, one that always fools me into thinking I'll do it more often. Yet the satisfaction of a finished loaf, served warm with salmonberry jam, is a small reminder that there *is* tranquility within the tasks of this way of life. It's a little like having multiple children under the age of six. Delightful, as long as you quit trying to get things done and just enjoy what's in front of you.

The other night we drove the muck truck, a bright orange mechanized wheelbarrow, down the trail to the beach. Liam rode inside, bumping along looking serious and loving every minute of it. We filled it with round black rocks to border a perennial bed, shaking tiny red spiders off the rocks first because of the superstition that they bring rain. The fact that there are millions of these sprinkle-sized spiders makes me wonder if it's more of a joke about Kodiak's 180 days of annual precipitation.

This time of night is almost always calm, as if some great mother has shushed the bay, tucking the mountains into shadows under soft clouds. I stopped to take a photo, probably the thousandth I've taken of this sunset, feeling grateful for the perfect evening, thinking about what we've made here and how the things this place denies us—the laziness of warm weather, the ease of appliances—do not equal more than the vast green and blue laid out before us. Though this contentment may be gone by morning, for now it seems so simple.

the outlaws of amook island

ONLY SIX MAMMALS are native to Kodiak Island—the short-tailed weasel, red fox, little brown bat, river otter, Kodiak brown bear, and tundra vole. I just learned that, for a while, raccoons lived here, wandering along the same beach where our cabin sits. Raccoons are excellent swimmers; they survive in deserts and mountains and wetlands. You would think that Uyak Bay, with beaches full of clams and mussels, would suit them just fine. But raccoons are synanthropes, which means they thrive around human populations, and humans are few and far between on this side of the island.

When legendary Kodiak bear guide Morris Talifson was interviewed as an old man, he said, "I've spent a good portion of my life in the wilderness, and I've enjoyed that. But I sometimes wish I could have had the company of more people along the way. I like people, and they aren't plentiful out here." Some days this bay feels lonelier than anywhere I've been. I think I expected to feel more at home by now, after half a dozen seasons here.

Maybe I like imagining raccoons on Amook Island because I'm a transplant too. Or maybe I'm just curious because I've never actually seen a live raccoon. I'd hear hissing or chattering in the night, some evening in August when it gets dark, and step onto the back porch, aiming a flashlight toward my compost bin. Beady eyes would flash defiantly, shining over small paws clutching eggshells or an apple core. Or maybe this would be a few years from now, after a couple good salmon seasons and I'd have the composter of my dreams—a big metal one that sits aboveground and turns with a handle, and there in the flashlight beam a raccoon would be stretched up on its toes about to open the composter door, little rascal.

I bet those raccoons wouldn't even need to scavenge in my compost. Someone would probably be feeding them just like people feed the deer around here even though the law forbids it. The caption of a 1943 Kodiak newspaper photo of Oscar the Eagle reads: "Favorite pet of many a Kodiak outfit is an Alaskan eagle, easily caught while young, a tame and friendly bird to have around." Oscar's talons are digging into his perch—a soldier's shoulder—and the soldier looks terrified.

Why do we do that, tame foxes and hang bird feeders? Why do we try to get friendly with wild things? Perhaps we're trying to feel more at home in wild places, to ease the inherent lonesomeness of big country. Or maybe we've seen too many movies about talking dogs and kind of believe most animals think in English and thank us properly with the best of manners. There's an ongoing feud in Kodiak between the man who feeds the pigeons (illegally) and the man who feeds those pigeons to the falcons he takes as fledglings from nests and raises as pets.

Raccoons are just one on a long list of attempted transplants on Kodiak. Russians introduced silver foxes to the archipelago in the 1700s, some of the earliest animal stocking in Alaska. Later, the territorial government encouraged the introduction of new species to expand hunting and trapping opportunities, and people tried everything from softball-sized partridges to six-hundred-pound muskoxen, with little thought given to the impact on native plants and animals. Only a few species like moose and mink failed to take. By the 1930s, nonnative populations of deer, elk, ground squirrels, beaver, and muskrat had been established on the Kodiak Archipelago. Sitka black-tailed deer introduced by the Alaska Department of Fish and Game have done so well that we tend to forget they don't really belong.

The 1890 Census reported, "A few hogs can be seen rooting about promiscuously, but as they feed entirely upon fish, mussels, and clams, their meat, with its strong fishy flavor, finds no favor with civilized palates." In more recent history, a local Kodiak character, Reed Oswalt, introduced a population of wild boars to nearby Marmot Island. These were joined by the occasional pig dropped off by 4-H families who couldn't bring themselves to slaughter their state fair projects (likely because all the movies they watched featured talking pigs).

Not every introduction was intentional. In 1805 Georg von Langsdorff described a maritime invasion of cockroaches: "The numbers were said to be so great that, while workers unloaded the ship and carried sacks of flour to the warehouses, they, like ants, built a living highway from the ship to the warehouses."

Invasive species are rarely a good thing, a belief reflected in current Alaska wildlife management policies. Yet even our Sitka spruce forests, a defining feature of Kodiak, began with invading trees carried here by ocean currents from Southeast Alaska. And occasionally transplants fall in the welcome category—the firewood from spruce trees offsets oil bills, and venison in the freezer lessens grocery bills.

Any corn farmer in Iowa would say it's crazy to feed or raise raccoons. In certain parts of the country, shooting coons is practically a boy's rite of passage. Kits might appear sweet and cuddly, but cute does not apply to a fifty-pound raccoon swimming out ahead of your dog, then turning, climbing onto the dog's head, and hanging on until your dog drowns. It happens. Raccoons hunt cats. They rip the heads off chickens.

In the 1970s, Johnny Morton, a local longshoreman, raised a pair of raccoons in Kodiak until they started fighting with neighborhood dogs and his buddy Park Munsey offered to take them. Munsey hauled the raccoons out to his bear-hunting lodge in Amook Pass because he thought they'd be fun for his five kids. Park Munsey was a jack-of-all-trades; he flew his own airplane, and during summer months the Munsey family entertained travelers from around the world. Peter remembers stopping by the lodge as a kid and marveling at ashtrays made from bear paws, a footstool made from an elephant's foot. Buried on this side of Uyak Bay are gold-mining tunnels, the wife of the local moonshiner, and nearby, the steamship SS *Aleutian*, which hit a rock in 1929 and rests two hundred feet below the surface of the bay. Decades-old peonies bloom at Munsey's Lodge every summer. I've been waiting years now for mine to flower.

Park Munsey had a permit for one tethered or penned neutered raccoon. Now, after almost forty years, no one seems to remember how many (unneutered) raccoons first arrived at the bear camp, whether their liberation was accidental or deliberate, or if Munsey expected the raccoons to go wild. At first, the raccoons lived in a pen outside. They took treats from the kids or from hunters' pockets, but the raccoons weren't exactly friendly. Park's son Mike, who now runs the lodge, told me, "You couldn't even hold them when they were young without them trying to bite you or wriggle away."

"We thought of them as pets, but they didn't think of themselves as pets," said Mike's sister Toni, who runs the Rendezvous Bar in Kodiak.

After they were freed, about a dozen raccoons stayed near the bear camp for handouts. They fought and raised a ruckus below the cabin. At times their crying sounded like a bawling baby underneath the floor. The Munsey kids coaxed them into the cabin with cheese and then the raccoons carried off shoes and pillows, anything they could get their paws on. Soon trappers around Uyak began catching raccoons. By 1973, wildlife management heard rumors of a growing raccoon population on the west side of Kodiak and worried they would spread across the island, killing off bird colonies as they went. A raccoon was found stealing from an outdoor pantry at a setnet site on Bear Island, ten miles from Munsey's by water, thirty miles by land.

So Roger Smith, a wildlife management biologist at the Alaska Department of Fish and Game (ADF&G), flew out to Uyak in December to encourage Munsey to "destroy the beasts." But after talking to Park Munsey, Smith wrote in a report that "short of stationing a man on Munsey's doorstep indefinitely there was only one way to get rid of Munsey's coons. If they were to be gotten rid of, Munsey would have to bait them in and do it himself." Smith told Munsey he wouldn't cite him for noncompliance of his permit if he would remove all raccoons that appeared at his homestead. Park Munsey brought in a single raccoon tail the following spring.

I don't blame Munsey for his reluctance. Raccoons have some endearing qualities. Their nimble paws can undo zippers and open doors. They have at least thirteen calls. The babies twitter like birds. After Sterling North wrote *Rascal,* a charming memoir about adopting a raccoon, an animated adaptation was so popular in Japan that it led to a thriving raccoon population from released imported pets. Even half wild, the raccoons' antics around Munsey's lodge were entertaining to watch. And this was the 1970s—the days of bald eagle bounties hadn't ended all that long ago, or the ranching practice of gunning bears down with a semiautomatic M1 mounted to a Piper SuperCub. Fishermen still shot every sea lion near a fishing net.

In the winter of 1977, trapper Bruce Swanson caught four raccoons on beaches in Uyak Bay. The following year, U.S. Fish and Wildlife asked the Kodiak branch of ADF&G to help them eradicate the raccoons from the refuge. Fish and Wildlife would provide food, lodging, and support services if Fish and Game would provide an "eradication specialist" to survey the coast to trap and/or shoot any raccoons they encountered.

The refuge manager wrote, "This eradication project would be a difficult assignment for the specialist. Removal methods are limited to trapping and hunting. The specialist should come with the expectation of staying for six months—December 1 through May 31—and living and working in a field cabin at Uyak Bay. The individual should be hardy, reliable and accustomed to adverse conditions."

In the end, the money for the project came from an animal control division out of Colorado. They sent someone up to teach Denny Zwiefelhofer, a biological technician with the Kodiak Fish and Wildlife Service, how to use the Havahart traps in spite of the fact Zwiefelhofer had been trapping for a decade. When I called him, I could hear a hint of the Midwest in his voice. As a boy, he ran dogs and hunted raccoons for corn farmers. They sometimes got a hundred in a single season. Those were enormous raccoons, fifty- to sixty-pounders. At first, Zwiefelhofer thought the traps provided for the project were too small, but it turned out that Kodiak's raccoons were scrawny. The biggest one they ever caught was only nineteen pounds, a male whose teeth were completely worn down.

On April 20, 1980, Zwiefelhofer and Don Simms, a Division of Animal Control employee from Sacramento, headed out to Uyak Bay. Their objective: complete extermination of the introduced population of raccoons from the Kodiak National Wildlife Refuge. They searched for raccoons for two days but found only one set of tracks about five miles south of Munsey's camp on the east side of Uyak Bay. Then they placed twenty-one live traps on well-traveled game trails approaching the beach. They used live traps because of fox, deer, and bald eagles in the area, but also because Park Munsey's cats couldn't resist the sardines used for raccoon bait. More than once, Zwiefelhofer pulled a Munsey housecat from a Havahart trap.

All of the raccoons were thin and all were caught on the same side of the bay as Munsey's camp. Their poor condition revealed that the population was not as healthy or widespread as predicted. Notes about the animals caught and killed read: "female raccoon, not pregnant—fur worn off, teats hadn't been suckled recently" and "pregnant—four approximately 40 day old fetuses." The details kind of broke my heart. Maybe because I've read that raccoons aren't nearly as solitary as was once thought and that groups of females gather from time to time to chitter, piling onto a heap for communal naps. I imagine their gatherings a bit like our setnetter picnics, where the women inevitably congregate and for an hour or two our numbers offset the maleness of this place, the swagger of adolescent crewmen, young sons hovering at the window every time they hear a chainsaw or a motor.

Trap damage was heavy when Zwiefelhofer and Simms pulled them in May. "Apparently at least one bear believed the Havahart traps were folding models, so he helpfully flattened and folded up several for us.... With less help from our large furry friends we may even have traps enough to continue after next spring," states the KNWR narrative report for 1980. Though they often took a skiff around the bay to scout beaches and muddy areas, they never found more tracks. When they left, a local trapper, Bruce Swanson, was hired to finish the job.

There hasn't been a raccoon sighting in Uyak Bay for decades. Denny Zwiefelhofer thinks the narrow gene pool of those original raccoons may have caused their eventual lack of fecundity. This is a bountiful place, but perhaps the beaches didn't provide enough food in winter months, or the raccoons couldn't compete with foxes. It's hard to know if the raccoons would have died off on their own, as transplanted populations have in other parts of the state. Maybe they couldn't make it in this bay without people.

Though I grew up in a village just over the mountains from here, when I moved to Amook Island with Peter I realized how little I knew about the wind and weather and tides that control so much of our days. I am still trying to learn. Sometimes I worry that I could put in thirty or fifty seasons and not feel like I belong. Yet wonders arrive in Uyak as often as the tides. The irises I found growing near the lagoon and nowhere else, the three mountain goats that swam up to our beach and walked away nonchalantly, the albino rainbows we see when the sun shines over fog so thick I marvel that my husband can find his way across the bay in an open skiff. Those things, or certain days when the sunlight skips so brilliantly over the water you can hardly look and yet you have to look, make me want to know this place and think of it as home.

As unlikely as it is that raccoons are roaming around the island, I know that next summer I'll think of them when I hear animals outside the cabin at night. I'll take a second look at the tracks on our beach, imagining some last enclave of furry bandits hidden in a Kodiak bay.

cardinal points

ON THE EVENING it floated into the bay, Peter tied up the skiff and came up to the cabin for binoculars. It looked like a giant floating bowling ball. Sunlight bounced off the round shape rising eight feet above the waterline, and Pete wondered if it was a water tank lost overboard. We took the skiff out to see it, motoring slowly, cautiously. There's something disconcerting about extremely large, unrecognizable objects on the ocean. After more than thirty summers here, Pete has seen countless things floating in Uyak Bay. He recently turned the skiff for a closer look at bears on the beach and, glancing down, saw a shark swimming alongside the boat. "What are the odds," he asked, "of seeing two of the world's greatest predators at the same time?" Once he passed an enormous tree floating perfectly upside down with its wide trunk and full set of branches just under the waves.

A whale. Freshly dead, a bloated humpback rocked in the current. The smell was like durian fruit, or cantaloupe left too long on a countertop. The rocking movement unnerved me. I kept scanning the ocean around us, for what? An angry mama? Orcas? He was floating on his back, white fins extended. It's hard to make sense of an upside-down whale. What had glinted like smooth obsidian from a distance was actually ridged and textured with barnacles and tubercles. He was softer than I expected when I touched his side. Then another wave set him rocking and I jerked my hand back.

All summer we travel around Uyak Bay to check the nets, deliver our fish, pick up mail, or visit other sites. Yet by the end of the season, it feels as though we travel only two directions, away from the island and back. Lodges in the bay advertise this wilderness with words like *pristine* and *breathtaking*. Equally true are words like *confining* or *unsettling*. At high tide, the ocean seals off our beach at both ends. After a few days on Amook Island, I am eager to leave the beach, but my relief as our skiff picks up speed never lasts very long. Deep water scares me.

Old stories are snagged in my memory, like that of the only survivor when the tender *Cougar* went down near here in July 1946. He clung to a fuel tank for twelve hours, watching as several people, desperate to stay above the waves, climbed the rigging of the sinking boat. One of them, a pregnant woman, had been on her way to Kodiak to deliver. He watched until the mast disappeared underwater.

Ever since my friend Jenny mentioned that when someone drowns in cold water they sink to the bottom and stay there, I can't stop picturing people standing on the ocean floor, lined up like pale marble statues in a museum corridor.

Like the boy and his grandfather who went for a skiff ride in our bay and disappeared, although the empty skiff was found floating. That day as Dave, a local fisherman and poet, searched for his son and his father, he mistook his own calls echoing off the cliffs, hearing "Dad!" as the cry of his only child.

Or the missing parents of the drowned baby found still buckled into the car seat. They were Russian Old Believers skiffing between Kodiak and Raspberry

Island. I see the mother's scarf and long, silky skirt swirling in the current below the surface.

Or the newlyweds who swam for shore when their skiff filled with water as they picked a setnet just 150 fathoms from the beach in Uganik Bay. A third crewman hung onto the net and was rescued. I imagine them hand in hand, having forgiven the other for kicking toward shore, for following.

It's an impossible scene. But so is the idea of a seventy-foot whale passing unseen underneath our skiff. Or the millions of salmon, invisible until they thrash in our nets. Hundreds of feet beneath Uyak Bay are shipwrecks and sharks, old engines and crab pots. I am blind to all we pass over.

Each time we drive out the road in Kodiak we pass Woman's Bay and the abandoned fishing boat, the *Saint Patrick*. Twelve crewmen, afraid of being trapped inside when the boat flipped and went under, tried to swim for land when the *Saint Patrick* foundered in a storm near Afognak Island. Only two made it. The boat never sank. It seems wrong that it's still visible in the bay. It should be buried and hidden, the same way I push these stories under and try to forget them. Except that every time we cross storm-black water I see them, feet cemented to the ocean floor, their arms loose in the water, a movement like beckoning.

ⓒⓒ

I felt bad leaving him out there, a lonesome shape under a darkening sky. For a few hours I kept getting out of bed, putting on my glasses to peer out the cabin window to see if the whale was still floating in the middle of the bay. By morning he was gone.

Peter found the humpback on a beach a half mile down from us. I'd been thinking about the whale all day. I wasn't sure why I felt possessive. We'd found him once and then he'd landed on our island. I say our island although we own only a small piece of land here, one layered with midden and bones, overgrown with nettles and brush—reminding me daily of the impermanence of ownership. He was a yearling, about thirty-four feet long. The color and texture of a tire with skin peeling off in strips like black electrical tape. He looked smaller on the beach and now I wasn't afraid, because he was on land.

"Poor whale, Mommy," Liam said. "We need to push him into the water."

"He's too heavy," I said.

"How will he turn into a new whale?" he asked.

I tried to think of what that meant to a three-year-old. I told him that bears and eagles would eat the whale and eventually the waves would wash the whale's bones out into the ocean. More whales would be born. At the setnet site, our sons live around death. We catch thousands of salmon commercially, and we kill much of what we eat—halibut, cod, deer, crab, octopus. Sometimes this seems like the right way to raise our boys. They are aware of the work of subsistence and I hope they respect it. Other days, I want to shelter them from death that I find troubling. How do you raise boys who don't shoot at squirrels or songbirds? I would like them to grow to be men with a healthy view of the natural order and the food chain, but I also hope they will be gentle men.

On Amook Island, our boots crunch daily over tide-line carnage. It isn't unusual to wake to beaches paved silver with candlefish, or coated with dead krill. We recently found thousands of tiny squid on our beach. They were milky white, about as long as a nickel, with big pearly sad eyes. They filled three tide lines. The squid weren't so much fragile as made for water, so that now, on the beach, they seemed deflated, their wide-open eyes giving them a look of astonishment.

I felt responsible because the night before, Liam and I had flattened boxes of milk on the beach. One milk container had leaked and the whole case smelled rotten. The milk had seemed fine, though, when we poured it into the ocean. The tide lapped at our feet, sweeping the milk south. I couldn't believe how far the white spread through the water. In the sunlight each curl of wave went aqua. I knew the squid hadn't been lured by milk. It was just that a bear lumbered by a few minutes after we'd finished, and I wondered if he'd been drawn to the white waves, and seeing him sniff at Liam's small footprints reminded me of how alone we are out here, how no one would hear me screaming.

"I have to be careful not to get hurt," I reminded myself, picturing baby Luke crawling toward the water as I lay unconscious from a fall. I tried explaining emergencies to our three-year-old.

"You would call on the radio," I told Liam.

"I'd call for a fireboat," he said. He was thinking of a Richard Scarry book we'd been reading.

"Maybe a boat would come," I said "Or maybe a helicopter." There are no roads to the cabin. There are no neighbors nearby. When Peter leaves to pick nets, I know it may be hours, a day, before we see him again.

⊚⊚

It felt like noon in the bright June light at 6:30 p.m. Pete had called on the radio a few minutes earlier. "The floatplane just landed. The tide is low enough you could probably get there on foot," he said. "You might have to scramble over a few rocks, but I think you could make it." As I rounded each corner of beach I caught glimpses of the orange-and-yellow floatplane.

Kate Wynn, a biologist, had flown out from Kodiak to gather DNA samples from the humpback and check for toxins. When I got there, they were cutting huge slabs of blubber from the whale with fillet knives that they had to keep sharpening. Kate was sweating. The whale's side looked like a piano missing keys. For each new rectangle, the size of a car windshield, three people pried and sliced and pulled with sharp hooks taped to long poles. It was odd to see this smooth, earthy shape carved into geometric triangles and rectangles. The blubber made a squeaking sound as it was peeled back. Nyeem, a fisheries student Kate had brought along, was playing with the barnacles on the whale. He dropped water onto the barnacles, watching as they opened and closed. Rather than set down her knife, Kate jabbed it into the side of the whale—like stabbing rigid Styrofoam—when she needed to walk around and give directions. Blood gurgled out of a fist-sized hole, making a slow hiss, like a punctured tire.

"Is Sara still here?" Kate asked. "You should see the fluke," she pointed with her knife. "This one's been tangled in net or rope before. Looks like he got through it."

I looked obediently at the scarred lines along his tail. I felt implicated. "Seiners catch whales as often as setnetters do," I thought. I sat down on a rock and set my hand down on a lump of whale gunk and then tried to rub it off in the sand. I would smell this for days.

The whale never seemed real. Not floating, or when we saw him perfect on the beach, or as the necropsy team hacked into him. I thought I should feel sad, but mostly I felt curious. Then as I got ready to leave—I was nervous about making it back before the incoming tide swallowed the beach—I saw the pale pink roof of his mouth. Like a kitten's tongue. It stopped me in my tracks. The color invokes delicateness, nursery rooms or peonies; it was startling to see it out of context. I respond in a similar way to photographs of small tangible items within a backdrop of natural disaster or wreckage—the child's shoe at the site of an accident, the infant piled onto bodies after an earthquake. It's not the grand size of oceans and mountains that troubles me, it's the scale of my life within this vast landscape. I am always aware of my smallness here, and being reminded of such frailty shakes my belief that as a mother I can protect the things I love.

The other day as we loaded mail into our skiff at the cannery, a girl I'd never seen before stood nearby. She was maybe nine or ten, small for her age. "There's lots of good skipping rocks," she said. She had a heart-shaped face, there were hearts embroidered on the back pockets of her jeans. She wore a pink knit hat, and eyeliner, mascara, and brown eyeshadow. The makeup made her look womanly, which was disconcerting because she probably weighed all of fifty pounds. It wasn't child pageant garish, but it seemed wrong in the setting, on a little girl throwing rocks into the ocean.

"My name's Stevie Lee," she said to Liam. I looked around for her parents. What I saw instead were men. At the cannery, on the dock, on the decks of fishing boats. And inside those fishing boats, dark bunks with stained sleeping bags and *Hustler* and *Playboy* magazines, men dreaming of pearl-white thighs, the longing that once made mermaids of seals and manatees. This girl drifted somewhere between awareness and innocence. I wondered when I had moved beyond both of those into distrust and apprehension.

She picked up a jellyfish. She'd gotten a disposable glove from somewhere and she held the jellyfish flat, like a glass plate on her blue-gloved hand and watched it solemnly. "It's breaking in half," Stevie Lee said. She slipped the jellyfish into the water as we pulled away from the beach on our skiff.

"Is it swimming?" I asked. "It looks like it's swimming."

"It broke in half. I think it's dead." She stared at me.

Of course it was dead. Why did I say that? I wanted to pretend she was young enough to pretend along with me. I wanted to stop the invitation of her pretty, made-up eyes. I watched her as we pulled away, until the mountains loomed up and distance erased her.

A Northeast. The storm gained momentum all day. It went from waves to whitecaps, from whitecaps to great thick swells. I followed my husband's skiff across the bay through binoculars. During storms, we call on the radio from either side when someone makes it across. I thought of my whale. When did I start thinking of him as mine? Kate had tied his fluke to the rocks with a shot of crab line. Will it hold him? I pictured him stripped and leaking, chunks of blubber carried to sea like rafts, crabs feeding while the barnacles bask in salt water. They will go down with their vessel.

Sea spray coated the cabin windows. Gusts of wind shook the walls. The laundry flapped wildly on the line. Pete and Liam were coming home across Uyak. My mother-in-law called on the radio to make sure I could see them. They should have turned back; several times I was sure Pete would turn the skiff around. My stomach churned. Waves flung the skiff upward, pointing the bow skyward before it slammed down into white spray.

"He wouldn't take chances with Liam in the skiff. They'll be okay," my mom said. She held Luke in the cabin while I ran down to the beach. I waited near the waves, feeling like the gusts of wind had thrown open a door inside of me—open to the strength of wind and sea, and to the years of worry that surge through a life, testing our ties to places and people.

It was too rough to bring the skiff in so Pete tied off on the running line. He shouted to me, but I couldn't hear him over the storm. He held Liam and jumped toward the beach, landing in water up to his waist. We struggled to pull the boat away from the rocks. My hands were shaking. Liam's chubby ankles were pink with cold.

"I should have turned back," Pete said.

The whale is still tethered. Some evenings we take the skiff by to look for bears. Their landslides and trails are all over the cliff, but I've never seen anything but tracks. The whale is sunken, mottled a corroded orange and white.

Its color fades by the day, a naked felled giant. Passing by you hardly see it. The whale has become part of the beach, like an old car rusting away on the edge of someone's property. When I think of the humpback now, I imagine its pale bones along our walkway, marking a path home.

acknowledgments

I WOULD LIKE TO GRATEFULLY THANK the following people for their generosity and kindness: Alaska writers Sherry Simpson, Eva Saulitis, Nancy Lord, and Peggy Shumaker. Thank you to James Engelhardt and the advisory board at the University of Alaska Press.

These essays were written in fragments of time over the last several years—late at night, during Liam's or Luke's naps, and days the boys spent with their grandparents, Walt and Kate Loewen and Pete and Jan Danelski. I am so thankful for your help and the countless ways you enrich our lives. Without the steadfast support of my husband, Peter, this book wouldn't be. Liam and Luke, my hope is that you'll grow up to be just like your dad—kind, patient, and wonderful to be around. Thanks to our amazing family: MaryBeth Loewen, Reuben and Rosalie Loewen, Jackie Danelski, and Carrie and Sean O'Day.

I am indebted to friends and relatives for their words of encouragement and insight: Nathan Fuller (you are one in a million), Megan Wiedel (an insightful reader and beautiful writer), Susan and Dana Reid, Jan and Jerry Miller, Jessica Olsen, Amy Komar, Evelyn Davidson, Cliff and Henrietta Graser, Cid Blase, Erin Harrington, Lyllian and Neil Ruegsegger, Adelia Myrick, Maxwells, Don and Marian Loewen, Joyce Ruder, Mary Menis. Thank you Kaela, Gerry, Fran, Patrick, Susan, Cort, and many more fantastic aunts, uncles, and cousins who would take several paragraphs to name.

This collection stemmed from my first years of motherhood, and I am daily thankful for a mom as gracious and inspiring as mine. I'm glad to be going through these sleep-deprived years with such wise, funny friends—fabulous moms, all—Misty Pekar, Kim Dorner, Jennifer Pederson, Stefanie Shanebrook, Kate Stewart, Heidi Osborn, Ana Hinkle, Jennifer Foster, Marie Acemah, Amanda Swanson, Melissa Gandel, Alexis Jackson, Balika Hakaanson, Theresa Miller, Zoya Saltonstall, Tricia Kovacs.

Thank you, Joeth Zucco and Shana Kelly, for your attentive editing. Thanks to Alf Pryor, Nat Nichols, and Natalie Trenery for sharing your photos, and to John and Philip Wohlstetter for sharing your stories. A big thanks to the Alutiiq Museum, the Kodiak Military History Museum, and to Katie Oliver and Anjuli Graham at the Baranov Museum for help with research questions.

I feel lucky to have learned from the talented faculty and writers in the UAA low-residency MFA program: David Stevenson, Anne Caston, Heather Lende, Kathleen Tarr, Richard Chiappone, Jo-Ann Mapson, Judith Barrington, Ernestine Hayes. Thanks to fellow MFA students—some of the first readers of several of these essays—Linda Ketchum, Joan Wilson, Jason Eisert, Kristine McRae, Jessica Graves, Eric Larson, Robi Craig, Scott Burton, Michael Dinkle, Andrea Nelson, Michele Robinson, and Lynn DeFillipo.

Many thanks to the editors and staff of the literary journals in which these essays first appeared: *Terrain, River Teeth, Laurel Review, Cirque, Motherhood Muse,* and *Literary Mama.* Several essays began as columns in the Anchorage Daily News. Thanks to my editors there, Julie Wright and Mike Dunham.

Heartfelt thanks to the community of Kodiak and to all of the fishing families in Uyak Bay—you make me glad to call this island home.

sources

The following selection of books and articles were helpful in writing these essays. I am indebted to Peggy Holm and Sue Jeffrey at the Kodiak College Library for their help, insight, and enthusiasm. Thank you to the staff of the UAA Consortium Library and Archives and to all of the Alaska libraries where I learned to love books.

GIANT WINGS
Angier, Natalie. "Sonata for Humans, Birds and Humpback Whales." *New York Times* 9 Jan. 2001, natl. ed.: F5.

Cousteau, Jacques-Yves, and Philippe Diole. *The Whale: Mighty Monarch of the Sea*. Trans. J. F. Bernard. New York: Arrowwood, 1972.

Ellis, Richard. *Men and Whales*. New York: Knopf, 1991.

Kelsey, Elin. *Watching Giants: The Secret Lives of Whales*. Berkeley: University of California Press, 2009.

Smith, Joshua. "Humpback Love Songs." *Australasian Science* (Jan.–Feb. 2010): 28–30.

Stewart, Frank, ed. *The Presence of Whales*. Anchorage: Alaska Northwest, 1995.

Winn, Lois King, and Howard E. Winn. *Wings in the Sea: The Humpback Whale*. Hanover: UP New England, 1985.

Witteveen, Briana H., Kate M. Wynne, and Terrance J. Quinn. "A Feeding Aggregation of Humpback Whales Megaptera Novaeanglieae near Kodiak Island, Alaska: Historical and Current Abundance Estimation." *Alaska Fishery Research Bulletin* 12.2 (2007): 187–96.

DECEMBER

Mishler, Craig. *Black Ducks and Salmon Bellies: An Ethnography of Old Harbor and Ouzinkie, Alaska*. Virginia Beach: Donning Co., 2003.

TO KNOW A PLACE

Anderson, Will. *Two Journeys: A Companion to the Giinaquq: Like a Face Exhibition*. Kodiak: Koniag, 2008.

Crowell, Aron L., Amy F. Steffian, and Gordon L. Pullar, eds. *Looking Both Ways: Heritage and Identity of the Alutiiq People*. Fairbanks: University of Alaska Press, 2001.

Haakanson, Sven. *Giinaquq: Like a Face*. Ed. Amy Steffian. Fairbanks: University of Alaska Press, 2009.

Holmberg, Heinrich Johan. *Holmberg's Ethnographic Sketches*. Ed. Marvin W. Falk. Trans. Fritz Jaensch. Fairbanks: University of Alaska Press, 1985.

Jeffrey, Susan M. *A Legacy Built to Last: Kodiak's Russian American Magazin*. Kodiak: Kodiak Historical Society, 2008.

Lantis, Margaret. "The Mythology of Kodiak Island, Alaska." *Journal of American Folk-Lore* 51.200 (Apr.–June 1938): 123–72.

Merck, Carl Heinrich. *Siberia and northwestern America, 1788–1792: The journal of Carl Heinrich Merck, naturalist with the Russian scientific expedition led*

by Captains Joseph Billings and Gavriil Sarychev. Trans. Fritz Jaensch. Ed.
Richard A. Pierce. Kingston, ON: Limestone, 1980.

Partnow, Patricia. *Making History: Alutiiq/Sugpiaq Life on the Alaska Peninsula.*
Fairbanks: University of Alaska Press, 2001.

HUNGER & THIRST

Andrews, C. L. *The Story of Alaska.* Caldwell, ID: Caxton, 1942.

Black, Dawn Lea, and Alexander Yu. Petrov, eds. and trans. *Natalia Shelik-
hova: Russian Oligarch of Alaska Commerce.* Fairbanks: University of Alaska
Press, 2010.

Black, Lydia. *Russians in Alaska, 1732–1867.* Fairbanks: University of Alaska
Press, 2004.

Chevigny, Hector. *Lord of Alaska: The Story of Baranov and the Russian Adventure.* Portland, OR: Binford & Mort, 1951.

———. *Lost Empire: The Life and Adventures of Nikolai Rezanov.* Portland:
Binford & Mort, 1958.

———. *Russian America: The Great Alaskan Venture, 1741–1867.* Portland:
Binford & Mort, 1965.

Crowell, Aron L. *Archeology and the Capitalist World System: A Study from Russian America.* New York: Plenum, 1997.

Davydov, G. I. *Two Voyages to Russian America, 1802–1807.* Trans. Colin
Bearne. Ed. Richard A. Pierce. Kingston: Limestone, 1977.

Dmytryshyn, Basil, E. A. P. Crownhart-Vaughan, and Thomas Vaughan, eds.
and trans. *The Russian American Colonies, Volume 3: A Documentary Record,
1798–1867.* Portland: Oregon Historical Society, 1989.

Engstrom, Elton, and Allan Engstrom. *Alexander Baranov, and a Pacific Empire.* Juneau: E. Engstrom and A. Engstrom, 2004.

Fortuine, Robert. *Chills and Fever: Health and Disease in the Early History of
Alaska.* Fairbanks: University of Alaska Press, 1989.

Golovin, Pavel N. *Civil and Savage Encounters: The Worldly Travel Letters of
an Imperial Russian Navy Officer, 1860–1861.* Trans. Basil Dmytyshyn and
E. A. P. Crownhart-Vaughan. Portland, OR: Western Imprints, 1983.

Hardwick, Susan W. *Russian Refuge: Religion, Migration, and Settlement on the
North American Pacific Rim.* Chicago: University of Chicago Press, 1993.

Hieromonk, Gideon, *The Round the World Voyage of Hieromonk Gideon: 1803–1809*. Trans. Lydia T. Black. Ed. Richard A. Pierce. Kingston: Limestone, 1989.

Huggins, Eli Lundy. *Kodiak and Afognak Life, 1868–1870*. Ed. Richard A. Pierce. Kingston: Limestone, 1981.

Khlebnikov, K. T. *Baranov: Chief Manager of the Russian Colonies in America*. Trans. Richard A. Pierce. Kingston: Limestone, 1973.

Miller, Gwenn. *Kodiak Kreol: Communities of Empire in Early Russian America*. New York: Cornell University Press, 2010.

Olson, Wallace M. *Through Spanish Eyes: Spanish Voyages to Alaska, 1774–1792*. Auke Bay, AK: Heritage Research, 2002.

Pierce, Richard A., ed. *The Journals of John A. Campbell and Frederick Sargent*, Kingston: Limestone, 1981.

———, ed. *Siberia and Northwestern America, 1788–1792. The Journal of Carl Heinrich Merck*. Kingston: Limestone, 1980.

———. *Russian America: A Biographical Dictionary*. Kingston: Limestone, 1990.

———, trans. *The Russian-American Company: Correspondence of the Governors Communications Sent: 1818*. Kingston: Limestone, 1984.

RaLonde, Raymond. "Paralytic Shellfish Poisoning: The Alaska Problem." *Alaska's Marine Resources*. Marine Advisory Program, University of Alaska. Oct. 1996. Retrieved online Mar. 2012.

Rezanov, Nikolai Petrovich. *Rezanov Reconnoiters California, 1806*. Ed. Richard A. Pierce. San Francisco: Book Club of California, 1972.

Sarychev, Gavrila A. *Account of a Voyage of Discovery to the North-East of Siberia: The Frozen Ocean and The North-East Sea*. Amsterdam: Da Capo Press, 1969.

Sauer, Martin. *An Account of a Geographical and Astronomical Expedition to the Northern Parts of Russia: For Ascertaining the Degrees of Latitude and Longitude of the Mouth of the River Kovima, of the Whole Coast of the Tshutski, to East Cape, and of the Islands in the Eastern Ocean, Stretching to the American Coast/ by Commondore Joseph Billings, in the years 1785 to 1794*. London: T. Cadell, Jun. and W. Davies, 1802.

Smith, Barbara Sweetland, and Redmond J. Barnett, eds. *Russian America: The Forgotten Frontier*. Tacoma: Washington State Historical Society, 1990.

Starr, Frederick, ed. *Russia's American Colony*. Durham: Duke University Press, 1987.

Taylor, Alan. *American Colonies*. New York: Penguin, 2001.

Tikhmenev, P. A. *A History of the Russian-American Company*. 1888. Trans. and ed. Richard A. Pierce. Seattle: University of Washington Press, 1978.

Von Langsdorff, Georg. *A Voyage Around the World, 1803–1807*. Ed. Richard A. Pierce. Kingston: Limestone, 1993.

A LAKE BY ANY OTHER NAME

Brodie, George K. *George K. "Steve" Brodie Papers, 1934–1941*. Archives and Special Collections, Consortium Library, University of Alaska Anchorage.

"Charles Wohlstetter's Many Careers." *Business Week* Aug. 1969: 36–41.

Donahue, Ralph J. *Ready on the Right: A True Story of a Naturalist-Seabee on the Islands of Kodiak, Unalaska, Adak and Others*. Kansas City: Smith, 1946.

"Lake Named Rose Teed by Army in Alaska: Engineers Mapping Area Find One with an Hour-Glass Figure." *New York Times* 29 Nov. 1942.

"Our Rose Gets Big Part in Famed Review." *Kodiak Bear* [Fort Greely, AK] 15 Jan. 1943. 1+.

Sholl, Cecil. "Gathering Around the Radio." *Elwani* 9 (1980): 19–22.

Smith, Edmund G. *Edmund G. Smith Diary, 1942–1943*. Archives and Special Collections, Consortium Library, University of Alaska Anchorage.

Wohlstetter, Charles. *The Right Time, the Right Place*. New York: Applause, 1997.

PACIFIC SANDWICHES

Beaglehole, J. C. *The Life of Captain James Cook*. Stanford: Stanford University Press, 1974.

Gilbert, George. *Captain Cook's Final Voyage*. Ed. Christine Holmes. Honolulu: University of Hawaii Press, 1982.

Hough, Richard. *The Last Voyage of Captain James Cook*. New York: William Morrow and Company, 1979.

Ledyard, John. *The Last Voyage of Captain Cook: The Collected Writings of John Ledyard*. Ed. James Zug. Washington, DC: National Geographic Society, 2005.

Pierce, Richard A. *Russia's Hawaiian Adventure, 1815–1817*. Kingston: Limestone, 1976.

Quammen, David. *The Song of the Dodo: Island Biogeography in an Age of Extinctions*. New York: Scribner, 1996.

Rickman, John. *Journal of Captain Cook's last voyage, to the Pacific Ocean, on Discovery: Performed in the years 1776, 1777, 1778, 1779, and 1780 A new edition, . . . from the voyage published by authority*. Ed. David Henry. London: Gale, 2010.

Williams, Glyn. *The Death of Captain Cook: A Hero Made and Unmade*. London: Profile Books, 2008.

WINTER IN JUNE

Clemens, Janet, and Frank Norris. *Building in an Ashen Land: Historic Resource Study of Katmai National Park and Preserve*. Anchorage: National Park Service, 1999.

Erskine, Nellie. Letters to her mother. 15 June–5 July 1912. T. S. Baranov Museum, Kodiak.

Erskine, Wilson Fisk. *Katmai: A True Narrative*. London: Abelard-Schuman, 1962.

Goforth, Pennelope. *Sailing the Mail in Alaska: The Maritime Years of Alaska Photographer John E. Thwaites, 1905–1912*. Anchorage: AK Cybrrcat Productions!, 2003.

Griggs, Robert F. *The Valley of Ten Thousand Smokes*. Washington, DC: National Geographic, 1922.

Schaaf, Jeanne M. *Witness: Firsthand Accounts of the Largest Volcanic Eruption in the Twentieth Century*. Washington, DC: National Park Service, U.S. Department of the Interior, 2004.

Schmidt, Gary, and Susan M. Felch, eds. *Winter: A Spiritual Biography of the Season*. Woodstock, VT: Skylight Paths, 2003.

Stevens, Gary. "The Valley of Ten Thousand Smokes." *Kodiak Daily Mirror* 30 Jan. 1985.

HOMETOWN ODE

Andrews, Carolyn Erskine. *Faraway Island: Childhood in Kodiak*. Portsmouth: Great Bay Press, 2000.

Burroughs, John, John Muir, et al. *Alaska, the Harriman Expedition, 1899*. New York: Dover, 1986.

Grinnell, George Bird. *The Harriman Expedition to Alaska: Encountering the Tlingit and Eskimo in 1899*. Fairbanks: University of Alaska Press, 2007.

SEA CHAINS BROKEN

Ashes and Water. Kodiak: Kodiak Historical Society, 1976.

Atwood, Evangeline, and Lew Williams Jr. *Bent Pins to Chains: Alaska and Its Newspapers*. Philadelphia: Xlibris, 2006.

Chaffin, Yule, Trisha Hampton Krieger, and Michael Rostad. *Alaska's Konyag Country*. Homer, AK: Chaffin, 1983.

Cohen, Stan. *8.6: The Great Alaska Earthquake*. Missoula, MT: Pictorial Histories Publishing Co., 1995.

Griffin, Joy, ed. *Alaska Earthquake 1964: Where Were You?* Homer, AK: Wizard Works, 1996.

Hume, Charles. "The Great Alaska Earthquake Wreaks Havoc in B.C. Too." *Globe and Mail*, Mar. 1964. Retrieved online 21 Mar. 2012.

Johnson, Thelma, Charles Madsen, Roy Madsen, Mary Cichoski, and John Reft. Recorded interviews. Kodiak Oral History Project. Kodiak, 1991. Audiocassette.

FIFTEEN TIMES OVER THE BRIDGE

Hutchison, Isobel W. *Stepping Stones from Alaska to Asia*. London: Blackie & Son, 1937.

RED CAVIAR

Jarvis, Norman. *Caviar and Other Fish Roe Products*. Washington, DC: Bureau of Commercial Fisheries, 1964.

Saffron, Inga. *Caviar: The Strange History and Uncertain Future of the World's Most Coveted Delicacy*. New York: Broadway Books, 2002.

THE OUTLAWS OF AMOOK ISLAND

Burris, Oliver E., and Donald McKnight. *Game Transplants in Alaska*. Juneau: ADF&G, 1973.

Department of the Interior Census Office. *Report on Population and Resources of Alaska at the Eleventh Census: 1890*. Washington, DC: GPO, 1893.

Kodiak National Wildlife Refuge. *Annual Report*. Kodiak: Kodiak National
Wildlife Refuge, 1980, 1981.

CARDINAL POINTS

Erskine, Wilson Fiske. *White Water: An Alaskan Adventure*. London: Abelard-
Schuman, 1960.

OTHER BOOKS ABOUT KODIAK AND ALASKA

Bancroft, H. H. *History of Alaska, 1730–1885*. New York: Ahtiguosian, 1959.

Chamisso, Adelbert von. *A Voyage Around the World with the Romanzov
Exploring Expedition in the Years 1815–1818 in the Brig Rurik, Captain Otto
Von Kotzebue*. Trans. and ed. Henry Kratz. Honolulu: University of Hawaii
Press, 1986.

Dodge, Harry B. *Kodiak Island and Its Bears: A History of Bear/Human Interac-
tion on Alaska's Kodiak Archipelago*. Anchorage: Great Northwest Publishing, 2004.

Ford, Corey. *Where the Sea Breaks Its Back: The Epic Story of a Pioneer Naturalist and the Discovery of Alaska*. Boston: Little, Brown, and Co., 1966.

Greely, A. W. *Handbook of Alaska: Its Resources, Products, and Attractions in
1924*. New York: Scribner, 1925.

Gruening, Ernest. *The State of Alaska*. New York: Random House, 1954.

Guimary, Donald. *Marumina Trabaho: A History of Labor in Alaska's Salmon
Canning Industry*. Lincoln, NE: iUniverse, 2006.

Moser, Jefferson. *Alaska Salmon Investigations in 1900 and 1901*. Washington,
DC: GPO, 1901.

Page, Roger. *This is Kodiak*. Kodiak, AK: Roger Page, 1982.

Roppel, Patricia. *Salmon from Kodiak: An History of the Salmon Fishery of Kodiak Island, Alaska*. Anchorage: Alaska Historical Commission, 1986.

Roscoe, Fred. *From Humboldt to Kodiak, 1886–1895*. Ed. Stanley N. Roscoe.
Kingston: Limestone, 1992.

Slocum, Victor. *Capt. Joshua Slocum: The Life and Voyages of America's Best
Known Sailor*. New York: Sheridan, 1972.

Studebaker, Stacy. *Wildflowers and Other Plant Life of the Kodiak Archipelago:
A Field Guide for the Flora of Kodiak and Southcentral Alaska*. Kodiak, AK:
Sense of Place, 2010.

Webb, Robert Lloyd. *On the Northwest: Commercial Whaling in the Pacific Northwest, 1790–1967.* Vancouver: University of British Columbia Press, 1988.

Will, Anne M. *A History of the City of Kodiak.* Anchorage: The Commission, 1981.

Willoughby, Barrett. *Alaska Holiday.* Boston: Little, Brown, and Co., 1942.

Wolff, Geoffrey. *The Hard Way Around: The Passages of Joshua Slocum.* New York: Knopf, 2010.

notes & photo credits

Map by Stefanie Shanebrook, who kindly agreed to dabble in cartography. It is meant to give a sense of locations specific to the essays in this book, which is why other bays and villages around the Kodiak Archipelago aren't labeled.

WOMAN OVERBOARD
The International Code of Signals used in this essay are found in Peter
  Kemp's *The Oxford Companion to Ships and the Sea*.

CAPACIOUS
The lines of poetry are from Li-Young Lee's "From Blossoms."
Photo courtesy of MaryBeth Loewen, 2008.

A LAKE BY ANY OTHER NAME

Rose Teed. Baranov Museum, Clevenger collection, P355-8-20. n.d.

ELEMENTARY LOVE

The teacher's name has been changed in this story.

Fourth of July Foot Race at Kodiak. July 4, 1915, uaa-hmc-0186-volume1-3554, National Geographic Society. Katmai Expedition. Album 1. Robert F. Griggs. University of Alaska Consortium Library Archives.

WINTER IN JUNE

Kodiak Refugees on the Manning, 1912, Baranov Museum. OP-600.

HOMETOWN ODE

Miss King Crab, 1967. Photo courtesy of Barbara Hellmueller.

SEA CHAINS BROKEN

Many of the accounts in this piece are taken from the Alaska Oral History Project through Kodiak College. The title references Bob Dylan's "When the Ship Comes In."

Kodiak Tsunami Photo. Alaska Earthquake Archives Committee Collection, 1972-153-218, Archives, Alaska and Polar Regions Collections, Elmer E. Rasmuson Library, University of Alaska Fairbanks.

FIFTEEN TIMES OVER THE BRIDGE

Photo courtesy of Nat Nichols, 2011.